TOTAL FOCUS

TOTAL
FOCUS

MAKE BETTER DECISIONS
UNDER PRESSURE

Brandon Webb
with John David Mann

PORTFOLIO/PENGUIN

Portfolio/Penguin
An imprint of Penguin Random House LLC
375 Hudson Street
New York, New York 10014
penguin.com

Most Portfolio books are available at a discount when purchased in quantity for sales promotions or corporate use. Special editions, which include personalized covers, excerpts, and corporate imprints, can be created when purchased in large quantities. For more information, please call (212) 572-2232 or e-mail specialmarkets@penguinrandom house.com. Your local bookstore can also assist with discounted bulk purchases using the Penguin Random House corporate Business-to-Business program. For assistance in locating a participating retailer, e-mail B2B@penguinrandomhouse.com.

Library of Congress Cataloging-in-Publication Data

Names: Webb, Brandon, author. | Mann, John David, author.
Title: Total focus : make better decisions under pressure /
Brandon Webb with John David Mann.
Description: New York : Portfolio Penguin, [2017] | Includes index.
Identifiers: LCCN 2017003387 (print) | LCCN 2017020544 (ebook) |
ISBN 9780735214637 (EPub) | ISBN 9780735214514 (hardcover)
Subjects: LCSH: Success in business. | Entrepreneurship.
Classification: LCC HF5386 (ebook) | LCC HF5386 .W349 2017 (print) |
DDC 658—dc23
LC record available at https://lccn.loc.gov/2017003387

Printed in the United States of America
1   3   5   7   9   10   8   6   4   2

Book design by Daniel Lagin

*Knowing the path and walking the path
are two very different things.
This book is dedicated to the
ultimate path walker:
the entrepreneur.*

Concentration is the secret of strength in politics, in war, in trade, in short, in all management of human affairs.

—Ralph Waldo Emerson, *The Conduct of Life*

Man's basic vice . . . is the act of unfocusing his mind, the suspension of his consciousness, which is not blindness, but the refusal to see, not ignorance, but the refusal to know.

—Ayn Rand, *The Objectivist Ethics*

Chase two rabbits, both will escape.

—Russian proverb

CONTENTS

❈ ❈ ❈

CONTENTS

TOTAL FOCUS

INTRODUCTION

✦ ✦ ✦

S taring through my scope at the man in my crosshairs, I take a slow breath. An Afghan farmer. An Afghan farmer with a rifle slung casually over his shoulder. A farmer who looks a lot like someone trying *not* to look like someone who's up to something he shouldn't be. I feel the pressure of my finger against the metal trigger.

Feel that pressure slowly increase.

January 2002. I'm standing sniper overwatch for my SEAL platoon as they approach a group of villagers in this mountain community in northeast Afghanistan for an exploratory chat. Everything seems cool. Everything looks innocent. Except for that farmer.

Something is off.

The thing is, these are Pashtun people, exactly the kind of people who, a few years from now and in this same region, will shield Marcus (*Lone Survivor*) Luttrell from the men trying to kill him. Our goodwill with these folks is a precious commodity, especially because we're out here in Taliban country. If I shoot this guy and it turns out he *is* as innocent as he's trying to appear, we can kiss that goodwill good-bye, and I will have to live with his blood on my hands for the rest of my life. But if I don't shoot him and it turns out he was up to no good after all, some of our guys could get hurt as a result. Hurt, or dead.

I can't call this in. There's no more intel to gather. It is what it is, and it's up to me.

I have a decision to make.

Do I pull the trigger?

I took a deep breath and looked down at my laptop. It was now twelve years later, and I was no longer in the service; I was sitting at the bar of the Jane Hotel in New York City, staring at an e-mail that held an offer to buy my business for $15 million.

Amazing, I thought. Considering that only a few years earlier, I'd been broke. No, worse than broke: with a negative net worth, because I'd owed nearly a hundred grand after my first business venture collapsed around me, taking all my life savings with it. And now here I sat, my new business barely two years old, and this big media company was trying to buy it from me. For $15 million. Amazing, all right. Still . . .

Something was off.

If I said yes, I would be $15 million richer, arguably set for life. It would mean I'd won. Right? But it would also mean the business I'd built with my own hands, for a community I cared about deeply, would no longer be in my control. And the people who'd built it with me: What would happen to them?

I couldn't call this one in, either. I had all the information I was going to have. There was no more advice to ask for or guidance to seek. It was what it was—and it was my call. I had a decision to make.

Do I pull the trigger?

Do I shoot the farmer?

Do I take the offer?

Both of these are decisions that, once made, can't be unmade. There's a lot of blood involved in one, a lot of money in the other. Both could affect the lives of a lot of other people, to say nothing of my own, for years to come. The two situations are different in a thousand ways, similar in a handful of ways, but identical in one.

They both require *total focus*.

Before I tell you the outcome of those two scenarios, I should probably give you my résumé. Here's the two-minute version:

— Tossed out of the house at the age of sixteen.

— Spent the first thirteen years of my adult life in the U.S. Navy, where I served in a SEAL platoon in Afghanistan immediately following 9/11.

— Back in the States, rose through the ranks of SEAL snipers to the top position as course master and helped redesign the entire SEAL sniper training program, the schoolhouse that produced a generation of legendary snipers including Marcus Luttrell, Chris Kyle (*American Sniper*), and a ton of others you've never heard of but who were just as effective on the battlefield.

— After leaving the service, traded my sniper rifle for a MacBook Air, signed up for a new career as an entrepreneur, spent the next few years going through business training in the school of hard knocks— years that were nearly as brutal as my time going through BUD/S (Basic Underwater Demolition/SEAL training) and the rest of SEAL training. Maybe more so. Raised millions of dollars and lost it all, my brainchild beaten to death by nuisance lawsuits in the California courts. Sat in my car on the La Jolla coast, staring out at the Pacific Ocean, and made the phone call to my lawyer that killed the business for good.

– Soon after which my wife filed for divorce. Full stop.

End of first minute

– After getting my teeth kicked in, forced to regroup and reinvent myself. Took a corporate job as an executive with a defense/aerospace company, where I was put in charge of $40 million in business related to a classified communications program. A cherry post, but with the blood of entrepreneurship coursing through my veins, I felt like a caged rat.

– To feed my creative side, accepted a writing job for a military Web site where I ended up running and hosting one of its most successful blogs, with millions of monthly viewers. Noticed that when it came to Special Operations content, there was a gaping hole on the Internet. You could read a book or watch a movie about Spec Ops, but there was no solid, legitimate source of information online. At least not until February 2012, when I left that post and founded SOFREP.com, a veteran-run Special Operations news site.

– Leveraging SOFREP's rapidly growing following, acquired and/or created additional sites and built these digital properties into Hurricane Group, Inc., which today is the fastest-growing military and outdoor content network on the Internet, reaching tens of millions of men monthly in over 220 countries through its Web sites, online TV, Internet radio, earned media partners that syndicate our content and link back to us, and our e-commerce clubs business.

– In the spring of 2014, received an unsolicited acquisition offer from Scout Media, backed by MTV founder Bob Pittman's private equity company, the Pilot Group, to purchase Hurricane for $15 million in stock and cash.

End of résumé

In the course of these two careers, I've realized something: the core principles it takes to achieve excellence in Special Operations are the same fundamental principles it takes to accomplish great things in business. Or for that matter in life.

It might surprise you to see a former Navy SEAL sniper writing a book on business. But it makes sense. The training, mind-set, and experience that go into building a Special Operations warrior are perfectly attuned to the sensibilities it takes to be an accomplished business owner and entrepreneur. In the SEAL teams, we're not taught simply to obey orders, as in other more conventional units. We're put into ingeniously brutal training environments that force us to fail, learn, adapt, and overcome, and in the process teach us to accomplish the mission, whatever it takes. We focus not on obstacles but on blowing through them with creative solutions. We are groomed to think fast, think for ourselves, and think unconventionally.

To make impossible decisions under insane pressure.

If soldiers and sailors are the military's version of a solid corporate workforce, we in Spec Ops are its entrepreneurs, innovators, and misfits. And the training we receive is powerfully effective in business, once translated and adapted for the business world rather than for armed conflict.

There's something about SEALs and other Spec Ops operators that leads a substantial number of us to start highly successful businesses. It's almost as if it were in our DNA. In *Total Focus*, I'm going to deconstruct that DNA and show you how you can develop it, too. In these pages, I'll describe a blueprint for success built on seven hard-won lessons learned from the crucible of war and re-learned on the battlefields of business. You might think of them as "The 7 Deadly Habits of Highly Successful People."

Each chapter illustrates one of these insights with experiences from my time with the SEALs, side by side with examples of how I've seen and experienced that same principle play out in the world of business. I'll also illustrate each with a profile of one exceptional entrepreneur from the circle of business professionals I've gotten to know in the last few years—people I've come to think of as "the Spec Ops warriors of the business world."

You're probably wondering, how did those two high-pressure decisions turn out?

I did not shoot the farmer. I reasoned that the risks of damage in taking the shot were higher than those in holding fire. The man likely never knew how close he was to death that day. Moments after I eased my finger off the trigger, I caught a glimpse of some character in Arab dress, out behind the village, hoofing it out of there and up a little goat trail, making his way for the Pakistan border as fast as his jihadist legs could take him. Damn. I'd been right. That farmer wasn't just an innocent dude, standing around; he was standing sentry, hiding the guy who escaped into the hills.

Had I made the right decision? Impossible to know, but I knew this for sure: all my guys were still alive.

And the $15 million offer? I turned it down. Sitting at the bar at the Jane in Manhattan, I typed out an e-mail that said, in essence,

Thanks . . . but no thanks. Two years later, I heard that a group of Russian investors had executed a hostile takeover of that same media group. A ton of the company's Web site producers resigned in protest, and a dozen tech people walked. It was a bloodbath.

I still have my company.

Chapter 1
FRONT SIGHT FOCUS

❖ ❖ ❖

Hi, Todd Dakarmen here—is this Brandon Webb, the SEAL sniper instructor dude? Look, I want to hire you to teach me how to shoot. How soon can you get up to L.A.?"

This guy didn't waste any time getting down to business. Before I'd even had a chance to say hello, or "Yeah, Webb, that's me," he'd laid out his agenda. The man wasn't shy about saying what he wanted, and he expected to get it.

I never did find out exactly how he got my name, let alone my phone number. Not that I was hard to find. This was mid-2011; two years earlier, when the Captain Phillips rescue mission happened and suddenly everyone was talking about Navy SEAL snipers, I'd been invited onto CNN to talk about the Naval Special Warfare (NSW) sniper training program my friend Eric Davis and I had helped develop and run for a few years. Ever since, I'd been in the public eye as an expert in sniper instruction. It would have been no challenge at all for a resourceful guy like Todd to track me down.

I hated to disappoint him, but I was already working out how to say no.

Those years teaching the sniper course were incredibly satisfying, and I still loved going out shooting with friends now and then. But private instruction was just not something I did. Besides, I was too busy.

Insanely busy.

Crazy busy.

"I've been working on my long-gun form," Todd was saying. "I'm not terrible, but I could be a lot better. I'd just as soon learn from the best."

It didn't feel right to just say no outright, but I figured that if I threw out a ridiculously high number, he would go away.

"I charge five hundred dollars an hour," I said. "Also, I charge half that rate, two fifty an hour, for my travel time to and from." From San Diego to L.A., that would've meant at least another fifteen hundred tacked onto my fee. Add that to the three or four hours I'd probably spend with him, at five hundred a whack, and his private shooting lesson was looking like close to five grand. I figured he'd tell me to go screw myself.

"No problem," he said.

Oh, shit, I thought.

What could I say? The man called my bluff. That weekend I threw some guns in the car and made the drive up to L.A. to take Todd Dakarmen shooting.

We spent the whole day at the range. He could shoot, but he hadn't been trained in how to set up his scope properly. I see this all the time, guys who get into shooting but don't realize how important the initial setup of the rifle is. It's like fitting a good business suit to the individual. You don't buy an expensive suit off the rack, throw it on, and go walk into your meeting. Everyone's unique: different inseam, different chest size, and so forth. If you want to look the part, the thing needs to be tailored; that's the only way it becomes *your* suit. The same thing applies to a good rifle. You could just throw on a scope and go shoot, but you're not going to get the best results. Ideally, you need to get down there, put your shoulder into the buttstock, gauge your reach forward, see exactly where your cheek comes to rest, adjust the distance from your eye to the scope, and so on. Everything matters. To do it right, to fine-tune a rifle so it fits you like a fine Hugo Boss, typically takes about an hour.

Todd had brought five rifles with him. We took the time to dial in two of them. Then we started shooting, working on his fundamentals. We took a break for lunch and then went back to shoot some more. I ended up staying the weekend.

While I was there, Todd took me out to his plant, a huge facility in a big industrial park in East L.A. There were smashed-up vehicles on the floor and racks and racks of auto parts stacked up everywhere, all carefully inventoried—all taken from wrecked Porsches. Todd and his wife run a business called Los Angeles Dismantler. They'll find a wrecked Porsche Turbo, worth maybe a few hundred thousand brand new, pay ten grand or so to the insurance company that's written it off, then dismantle it and resell the parts to specialty stores and individuals for ten or fifteen times what they paid for the wreck. Talk about a business model.

The following weekend, I went up to L.A. to give Todd some more private classes. This time, as we were having lunch, he asked me what I was up to these days, and I told him about all the different things I had going.

I'd been out of the SEALs for five years at this point. My first year out, I'd done some contract security work over in a country I won't name (it rhymes with "Barack") for a government agency, but other than that I'd been a strictly private-sector entrepreneur. For most of those five years, I'd been working on a multimillion-dollar land development deal, a massive training facility and race car track out in the Southern California desert, called Wind Zero. I was also an active investor in Neptunic, the company that created the Sharksuit (metal mesh protective diving gear). I was doing a bunch of consulting. I was writing for a few military Web sites. I was also working on my memoir, *The Red Circle*.

I had a lot going on.

Todd didn't say a word as I ran down my list, just ate and listened. Finally, when I'd gotten to the end of a paragraph and paused to take a bite, he sat back and looked at me.

"You know, when I look at you, I see a lot of myself in you." I took that as a hell of a nice compliment and was about to say so, but he kept going. "You're kind of a mess, you think?"

Not what I was expecting him to say.

"I was doing like you're doing, not too long ago," he went on, "going in every direction at once. One day, a mentor sat me down and said, 'Todd, you need to collect yourself and focus on one thing. You're all over the map. As soon as you focus, things will start coming together. And you'll be successful.' I took his advice. He was dead right. Once I focused on this one opportunity, on Porsche parts, big things started happening."

He pushed back from the table.

"Anyway," he said as we got up to go shoot some more, "think about it."

I did. He was right; I was all over the place. I had twenty different irons in the fire. I wasn't focused. It was a recipe for disaster.

And disaster was exactly what I'd cooked up.

That land development project had blown up in my face. The county had approved it, and it had a lot of local support, but at the eleventh hour the thing had been nailed shut and screwed to the floor by a nuisance lawsuit by the Sierra Club. We'd spent millions our investors had put up to get this far. Fighting the suit would have cost millions more. I was trying everything I could think of to salvage it, in talks with another developer to take it over, but it was crushing me. My marriage was in trouble, too.

Todd was dead on target. I wasn't focused. And because I wasn't focused, nothing was really coming to fruition.

The thing was, *I already knew this.* Learning how to focus was a critical part of my training as a SEAL sniper, and SEAL training isn't like a weekend seminar. The things they teach you in the SEAL teams, they go bone deep, and they never leave you.

In the teams, we called it "front sight focus," and it was as critical to survival as breathing.

"Brandon!" Cassidy hisses in my ear. "You're gonna have to Kentucky windage this thing!"

Lieutenant Cassidy and I and two other teammates are pinned like bugs to the scrubby Afghan mountainside; a knot of armed Taliban fighters are walking in our direction. They haven't found us yet, but they will any moment. If we leap to our feet and try to shoot it out, we're dead. Our only option is to call in an air strike and take these guys out with a bomb. Preferably without taking ourselves out at the same time. To call a strike with that degree of accuracy, someone needs to give the guys in the B-52 somewhere a mile or so above our heads the precise drop coordinates. That someone is me.

But because we weren't supposed to be out here in the first place, in this mission that was supposed to take eighteen hours but is lasting for days, I don't have my usual equipment with me: laser range finder, GPS, sniper scope, and the rest. All I have is my eyes, ears, brain, and gut.

As a sniper, I've been taught to estimate distances on the fly, but normally we're talking about shooting a bullet roughly the size of my forefinger from the muzzle of a rifle. Here I have to shoot a thousand-pound "bullet" out of a 125-ton aircraft, flying unseen somewhere over our heads at near the speed of sound, at a target less than five hundred yards away from where we are crouched. Without any range-finding equipment to help me aim the shot. In other words, I have to wing it, which is exactly what Cassidy means by "Kentucky windage." I have to get this right, and I have only seconds to do it. Sighting upward on an irregular rocky incline. In the deceptively vague light of daybreak.

Talk about an impossible decision under insane pressure.

Oh, great. Now the shooting starts. They've seen us. We're returning fire.

All right, class, let's review.

There are a bunch of guys shooting at us with intent to kill. We're in weird, crappy light, sighting uphill, with no sighting or range-finding equipment. I need to figure out exactly how far away these guys are so a plane somewhere up in the sky can drop a bomb on them and not hit us. And the guy in that B-52 is waiting for my numbers, *now*.

This is a situation that requires *focus*.

Focus. Yeah, I knew what Todd Dakarmen was talking about. Not only did I already know this; I had *taught* this. As a sniper, I had *lived* it. I just hadn't been applying it to my life in business.

I would never make that mistake again.

The Single Most Important Principle

Front sight focus is that state of intense concentration in which all your resources and abilities are brought to bear on a singular intention, when you're so locked on to the crosshair reticle inside your scope (or, in an iron sights system, the sighting device at the front of your weapon, hence *front sight focus*) that everything else blurs and disappears. There may be helicopters overhead, gunfire in the streets, someone inches away screaming at you, but to you none of that exists. It may be raining or snowing, boiling or freezing. Hell, there may be snakes or scorpions slithering over your leg. Inconsequential. Irrelevant. Everything about your surroundings slips far away into the background, and you are completely calm and relaxed, focused on that solitary objective.

What makes this even harder is that you still have to *know* all that chaos going on around you. Some part of your brain has to stay acutely aware of it all. (That's the subject of chapter 2, "Total Situational Awareness.") You never fully let go of it, not for a millisecond. You've just trained yourself to tune it out and stay in total focus.

I call that central area of total focus my "red circle"—hence the title of my first book—and it's as critical to business as it is to Spec Ops warfare.

I talked recently with a friend who runs a graphic design business. "I have this great business idea," she told me. "We'd create this virtual concierge service for people visiting New York City who need anything—a good restaurant reservation, dry cleaning, a manicure, whatever. Start here and take it to other cities. I think the idea's killer," she added, "but I can't do it on my own. I need a partner."

Here we go again, I thought. Probably just what Todd Dakarmen thought that first day we talked. The truth is, hers wasn't a bad concept. It may even be a good one. I think there's something there. But is it something she should pursue? And if she does, what happens to the design business?

If you can't pour yourself 100 percent into an idea when you start it, then you're starting it half-assed, and you'll never have more than a half-baked plan. When you have a half-baked plan, you can't expect any more than a half-baked outcome.

By nature, most entrepreneurs have some form of attention deficit disorder. It can be an asset, that spark-and-shoot creativity, but unchecked, it can also be a serious liability. I run into younger entrepreneurs all the time who tell me, "Yeah, I've got three startups going," and I don't need to hear any more, because I already know how that story ends. You may think you're going to do three or four things at once and keep that up until one of them shows itself to be the winner—but you're kidding yourself. All you're doing is shortchanging all three or four projects. You need to choose one. Not two. One.

Which one? Of all the great projects you could be working on, which one most merits your undivided attention? There's no definitive, one-size-fits-all approach here, because every person and situation is unique. It may be the one that makes the most sense for your circumstances; the most marketable; the one that taps into your greatest skills; the one that most touches your imagination, quickens your pulse, stirs your soul; the one you've been talking about for the last ten years but never let yourself dive into; or even the one you're most afraid to try. Whatever it is, the best I can tell you is this: once you start asking the question, honestly and earnestly, you'll know the answer. It's *that* one.

If I had to pick a single core principle for success in business, it would be this: choose one thing, focus on that one thing, and execute it to the absolute limit of your abilities. Focus on your career, invest in yourself, and learn how to say no to everything else.

Once you reach the point where you have the financial capacity to hire out or partner with the talent and team power to manage a range of different areas, you can start adding additional projects to your portfolio . . . *maybe*. If you're Richard Branson, or Elon Musk. And I've seen business owners who *aren't* billionaires do it, too. But it's a high-wire act and definitely not something you want to even think about until your own business is performing at the level you want it to, and doing so solidly and reliably. It's so easy to lose your focus.

This is job 1: Stay on task. Stay on target.

Stay focused.

Live Every Day with a Single Bullet

You've probably heard about BUD/S, the brutally difficult seven-month SEAL selection course. Maybe you've even seen footage of it, with men running along the sand carrying a gigantic log on their shoulders, or being sprayed with high-powered hoses, or doing calisthenics for hours in the freezing surf. My BUD/S class started out with 220 students; seven months later, there were fewer than two dozen left. So, yeah: it's as bad as it looks.

Sniper school was worse.

It's hard to fully explain just how torturous, how difficult, how stressful SEAL sniper school is. What makes it even harder to explain is that the stress is 90 percent mental. Hour after hour, day after day, you're placed under the most demanding conditions and expected to deliver on the most complex tasks, to the most exacting specifications. It's mentally and psychologically grueling. And for me, the single most grueling, difficult, torturous aspect of the class was an exercise we executed first thing every morning.

They called it "cold bore."

The concept of cold bore was simple: you wake up at dawn, go straight out onto the range, and fire a single shot, hitting whatever target they tell you to hit. The idea was to simulate conditions on the battlefield, when you won't necessarily be warmed up and ready, won't be prepared, won't know what's going on until the split second it's in motion.

Miss your cold bore target three days in a row, and you were out of the course.

How do you set yourself up to successfully make that shot every morning? Do you run out to the range as fast as you can, so you'll have more time to line up the shot, but then be out of breath? Or go at a more measured pace, keeping your breath under control so it won't screw up your shot, but as a result get there with no prep time? Nobody's at his best right when he wakes up, not even SEALs; so do you set your alarm and get up earlier, but then make yourself even more sleep deprived than you already are?

There's no way to win here.

And a cold rifle behaves differently than a warmed-up rifle. Shoot even three or four rounds through that bore and the metal heats up, which means the ballistics of your round changes. But not here, not with a cold bore shot. Great: sleep-soaked body and nervous system, cold and unpredictable rifle. For that matter, even a cold bullet will behave differently than a warmer round.

So I would sleep with my bullet. It was the one thing I could control. Every night, I took that single round to bed with me and slept with it like a long-lost lover.

The first day, I missed my shot. The second day, I missed my shot. I never missed again.

Today, more than a decade and a half later, I still wake up every morning with the sense that I've got that single live .300 Win Mag round under my pillow. And you might see me in a coffee shop in SoHo, or boarding an early flight at JFK, or heading into some Manhattan TV studio to do a morning interview on the latest foreign-policy development, but in my mind I'm out on that range getting ready to put my single round into the center of that target.

My parents used to say, if you're going to do something, make the effort to do it right the first time. Cold bore taught me that the first time may be the only chance you get. You don't always get to warm up. You don't always get to take practice shots. You can't always recover from a first-shot miss.

This is why you need to operate your business with front sight focus: every day you may be called upon to make a decision that will make or break your business, even make or break your career. Every day, you may be presented with conditions you're not prepared for, situations you haven't predicted, choices you don't have time to think through. Situations where you have one round to fire, and only one round, and cannot afford to miss.

Even on those days when those high-stakes challenges *don't* present themselves, if you operate in a way that anticipates them, if you go through your day with that single bullet in your pocket, you'll be operating at a level that sets you apart and primes you for success.

Embrace a State of Healthy Obsession

Putting a copper-jacketed high-speed sniper round into a target at one thousand yards—ten football fields away, far enough that you can barely see it with the naked eye—is an extremely complex task. Between point of release and point of contact, there are an enormous number of physical and environmental factors that mess with your round's flight path: wind currents pulling it right or left, air friction slowing it down, gravity dragging it downward. The time of day, how hot or cool it is outside, will have an impact on the round's velocity as it spits out the end of the barrel, which will have an impact on the shape of its arc as it travels. A spinning object's natural tendency to precess after a while—the way a spinning top will start to wobble as it slows, then spin out and fall—applies to a spiraling rifle bullet, too. In some cases, even the earth's spin can have an impact on exactly where that round hits when it reaches the thousand-yard mark.

In other words, there are a thousand things that can go wrong. Yet in our SEAL sniper course, we trained our students to place that round on the target, with dead-on accuracy, in shot after shot after shot, never missing.

If you think that takes a "steady hand," you're kidding yourself. Painting the trim in your living room takes a "steady hand." What being a Spec Ops sniper takes is a highly unusual state of mind—the ability to hold on to dozens of variables at the same time and bring them all together with a precision attainable only through something like a state of self-hypnosis.

Succeeding in business takes the same thing. Sit down with

twenty different successful entrepreneurs and have twenty different conversations. You'll hear twenty different stories, twenty different sets of circumstances, twenty variations on a theme. But there is one thing I guarantee you will hear in common: every single one of those twenty individuals will exhibit a level of engagement with his or her business that borders on the obsessive.

In fact, let's call it what it is. Because it *is* obsession. Not an unhealthy obsession, one you can't control, but an obsession born of passion and total dedication. Focus taken to a level that can seem uncanny, almost pathological. But it's not pathological. What you're seeing is the same thing you observe when you watch Lang Lang play the piano or Michael Phelps race to an Olympic gold medal. It's the inspired and inspiring capacity of human beings to transcend their limitations and do something great.

Not to make it all sound too grandiose. I'm not saying you have to be the Michael Phelps of the business world to be successful. Just that it's that same level of passion, transformed into focus, that creates something new, that works. That hits the target you're shooting for.

Win First in Your Mind

After I got back from Afghanistan in 2002, my BUD/S mate Eric and I were tapped to rework the SEAL sniper course from top to bottom, to bring it up to speed for the new century and new face of asymmetrical warfare. In completely revamping the course, we brought in all sorts of innovations, including new technologies, new curricula and teaching content, new teaching methodologies, and a new mentoring system. But of all the innovations we brought to the program, the one that I believe made the biggest difference in the caliber of our graduates was also the one that has the most direct relevance to achieving outstanding performance in business: our program of mental management.

Based on the performance practices of Olympic athletes and world-class shooters, the program focused on developing the two traits common to every one of these top performers: complete and total confidence ("I will win no matter what"), combined with rigorous, consistent, meticulous mental rehearsal ("and this is exactly what it will look like and feel like"). The first session we ran with this program in place, we had one shooter-spotter team shoot perfect 100s on the first part of a shooting test. Guess how often that had happened before. Never. The second part of the test, they shot a 95. Taken together, it was the highest score in U.S. Navy SEAL sniper course history.

Jack Nicklaus used to say that 90 percent of a tough shot is the mental picture you create and how you set it up and 10 percent is the physical swing itself. In that respect, sniping is a lot like golf. So is business.

Sun Tzu was right: the outcome of the battle is typically determined before the first shot is fired. I've seen businesspeople with all the advantages and opportunities in the world blow it because of what was going on behind their eyebrows. And I've seen guys with nothing, nothing at all but a mental picture of their own success, surprise everyone and transform industries.

Some people call this process "visualization," but I prefer the term we used in our sniper course: "superior mental rehearsal." Yes, part of that is to visualize your desired outcome, to fix your goal clearly in your mind. But it's more active than that. Just seeing the outcome is static. We taught our students to play out the scenario fully in their heads. You want your service to have a million unique visitors per month by the end of the year? You want your product in the hands of 100,000 satisfied customers? See it. Rehearse it.

Close your eyes and shoot a movie in your head, a moving picture of satisfied customers using your product. Picture your operations team handing you the year-end report with the million uniques or seeing your company listed on the *Inc.* 500 fastest-growing companies list. In your head, give your year-end talk to a gathering of your employees, thanking them all for working together to reach this phenomenal benchmark. You don't get to the top of Mount Everest unless you've already visualized yourself being there.

Today I live an extremely busy life, but I put aside the time to meditate every day. For me, meditation is something like a long hot shower, a quiet time and space that creates clarity of mind and fosters new thinking. Some of my best ideas come to me during meditation. It also exercises the muscles of the creative mind and helps create the blank canvas upon which I practice my mental rehearsal. I know my business plan, and I use visualization and mental rehearsal as reinforcement tools for elements within that plan. I'm winning in my mind.

If I need to overcome some self-limiting pattern or bad habit I've noticed, or if I'm looking to cement a new goal into my mind, I'll write it down—either the goal or a positive habit that is opposite of the bad habit—then place it in key places so I bump into it throughout the day, triggering my mental rehearsal again. When you do this, you're imprinting that positive idea or goal by forcing yourself to think about it.

At one point, I really wanted to get better at remembering

people's names. Each name I wanted to remember, I repeated it aloud three times and came up with a funny story I associated with that person, to lock it into my memory. Then I wrote down, "You are excellent at remembering people's names." I put a few slips of paper with that written on it around my home. After a week, I removed the slips; a week is all it takes. Now I'm good at remembering names.

I even block out specific time in my calendar that is devoted entirely to examining my current thoughts: time to put the cell phone away and read, think, focus on my personal and business goals, and build the thoughts I want to build. I've been doing this for a few years now and found it to be a very powerful thing.

My SEAL Team Three friend John Zinn started a company with a friend after getting out of the service, building armored vehicles that could withstand the rigors of the urban battlefield. At one point, they needed to bring out a second generation of vehicles but didn't have the capital to build a functioning prototype. They needed investors but couldn't get them without showing the prototype that they couldn't build. A no-win situation, right? Only in the physical world. To a SEAL, there is no such thing as a no-win situation, because you can always win in your mind.

John set up a large black box in the center of his company's showroom floor. When people asked what was in it, he said, "Oh, we can't show you that yet. That's Gen 2—very hush-hush."

Potential investors went nuts with curiosity. They had to know what was in there. John wouldn't say. Before long, John and his partner had gotten all the investment money they needed. They developed and distributed the new generation of vehicles, to great success.

Of course, there had been nothing in the box—no prototype, no nothing.

Only that's not really true, because there *was* something in there: *what John saw* was in there. He saw it so strongly that his potential buyers saw it, too, and laid down hard cash for it. Of course, hucksters do this, too; they're so good at painting the picture that they make you believe it, and you give them your money, and you get nothing. The difference was, John could deliver, and he did.

Pay Attention to Your Self-Talk

Next time the Olympics are on, pay attention to the interviews with the top-performing athletes, the ones who bring home the gold. You'll hear how they talk about their events and their training, the phrases they use, the words they feed themselves—how they literally talk themselves into success. Physically, these men and women train and train and train, just as SEALs do, but what sets the gold medalists apart is superior state of mind.

This is *not* something you're born with. It's something you develop, which means that no matter who you are, it's something *you* can develop. It just takes commitment, will, and practice.

As I said, when we studied Olympian gold medalists in the course of redesigning our sniper training program, we found two traits that set these superachievers apart. The first of these was *complete and total confidence,* and self-talk was how they created that total confidence.

If you think this sounds like some airy-fairy "personal growth" workshop talk, think again. Adopting this as one of our core training planks allowed us to turn out a generation of lethal snipers on the battlefield. We trained our instructors to teach and reinforce with positive language rather than negative, reminding students what *to* do and how to do it right rather than cautioning what *not* to do and castigating them for what they did wrong. And we trained our students in how to talk to themselves.

The truth is, whether out loud or silently, consciously or not, we all talk to ourselves constantly. Every one of us has this running commentary going on in our head. Most of us just aren't aware of it. The first step in training your self-talk is to become aware of that running commentary. Once you do, you will be amazed. I've trained myself to hear it, and I am constantly stunned by the crap people tell themselves.

I saw this happen in BUD/S. It was the middle of Hell Week, that legendary five-day ordeal designed to extrude all but the toughest from the program. During a rare lull in the punishment when we were allowed to eat something, I overheard two guys in the class talking.

"You know," said one, "I really wanted to be a pilot anyway."

"Yeah," said the other. "Did I tell you my girlfriend was hoping we would get married this month? It's tough, all this time away. I'm thinking this really isn't fair to her."

I could not believe what I was hearing. These guys were literally talking themselves out of making it through BUD/S! Right then and there I knew: when graduation came I would be standing there, and those guys would not. Months later, that's exactly what happened.

I saw and heard it happen again and again.

"Man, my leg hurts. I don't think I can do this."

"Someone's going to get killed, and I sure as hell don't want it to be me." At least this one was honest.

"All the cursing—it's just too much or me." Wait—was he *serious*? He was. I actually heard an officer in my BUD/S class say this, and sure enough he quit. So did all the others. Of the nearly two hundred men who quit my class before it was over, not one was *physically* incapable of making it through the course. They quit because they *decided* to.

Outstanding success starts in your mind, and so does failure.

I'm sure you've seen this, too. You have friends who talk to themselves this way, who say, "Oh, I'm just an average golfer," or "I'm not that good a swimmer," or "I'm not a people person," "I don't really dance," "I'm not good at math," "I'm not much of a businessperson," "I don't really know how to cook," and on and on. Maybe you talk to *yourself* that way. (Most people do.) If you're having that conversation with yourself, you're setting the bar too low. You're limiting yourself from ever becoming anything above average. You're talking yourself out of the success you want.

I mentioned that I meditate every day. I also rigorously monitor my self-talk. I remind myself continually that I'm going to achieve the outcome I'm shooting for, that I'm totally capable of achieving it, and that it's already in process. That it's inevitable. If that sounds like self-hypnosis, well, in a way it is.

We're all doing it anyway, every day. Every human being does. Why not do it intentionally and aimed in the direction you want? Building your victory up, instead of tearing it down?

Master Distractions

When Eric and I ran the sniper course, we had guys shooting targets at a thousand yards with loud music blaring at them, trash can lids banging together, the targets moving when they weren't supposed to. We did anything we could do to screw with their concentration. Not because we were trying to flunk them, but because we were trying to save their lives when they were in situations just like the one I faced on the Afghanistan hillside.

We had one particularly difficult drill we called the edge shot. We'd place all the students at eight hundred yards and inform them that their targets would appear in the vicinity sometime within the next three hours. This meant those SEALs might spend as much as three hours on the scope, concentrating and waiting. There was one student who diverted his eyes from his line of view for just a moment, just long enough to wipe the sweat from his brow—and when he looked back up, he saw his target disappearing from view. I still remember his anguished cry: "Noooooo!" He received a failing grade. A little sweat and discomfort is no reason to lose your focus.

High-pressure situations occur just as often in business as they do in combat, and while bullets and bombs are not involved and lives are not literally on the line, the stakes can be high. As a CEO, I consider it an invaluable gift that I've been trained to remain calm under fire. It has also helped me model behavior for the rest of my team; they know I expect cool heads during stressful times.

Distractions come in a thousand forms, and every one of them wants to tear apart the fabric of your focus.

I was going to make this heading *"Ignore* Distractions," but that's not realistic. Some distractions are nothing but noise, and you can completely ignore them, but there are plenty that you can't ignore, because there's something meaningful behind the noise. You can ignore hecklers and dream stealers; you can't ignore the threat of a lawsuit. You can ignore the critics who are just taking cheap shots, but you can't dismiss criticism altogether, because some of your most valuable learning is going to come from criticism. It's crucial to have an open mind and cast a wide net when it comes to what you're learning, hearing about, noticing. But some things are plain distractions, and you can't afford to give them an inch or a minute. I can't tell you which is which. You'll have to discern. What I can tell you is to make it a constant practice to ask yourself the question and exercise the judgment: Is this worth my time? Is this important? Is it important *to me*? Is it going to move my business forward or make me a better businessperson?

A hundred things will crop up in a day that you have to put some attention on. The trick is not to let them get in the pilot's seat. You're the one flying this plane, not them. You can't ignore them; you *can* master them. If you don't, they'll take your plane down.

The most tempting distractions, and therefore the most dangerous to your business, are those opportunities that you could easily see yourself getting engaged in. Things you *know* you could do a job of. Don't chase down rabbit holes. I get these coming at me constantly: projects I could be part of, ventures I could invest in, boards I could sit on. I'm not saying never. But my default mode is no.

Communicate Effectively and Efficiently

You've heard people say "time is money." What utter horseshit. Money is just money. You can always get more of it. But time? Time is the *opposite* of money. You can't put it in a savings account or invest it in a high-yield hedge fund. You have exactly the same amount of it as the poorest person on the planet, and you're never going to get more.

If you want to experience the mental equivalent of a naked dive into a freezing mountain lake, print out a list of all the calendar days from today until your hundredth birthday: you'll find it fits on the back of your office door. It's a sobering exercise; it sends shivers up my spine just to type the words. Your entire life, and you can flip through it in the blink of an eye. Wasting money is foolish, but it's something you can learn from and recover from. Wasting time? That's like cutting off a limb.

Time is the master of everything. Time will eventually put an end to all things—birds, trees, flowers, mountains, and, yes, your business. It grinds stones to sand and years to memories. Yet as terrible as it is, it's also the most beautiful thing we have. And while it is the master of everything, here's something truly amazing: *you* can master *it*.

I pack a lot into every twenty-four hours, and the way I do it is by staying clear on my focus, mastering distractions, and paying attention to the quality of my communications.

People who communicate regularly with me soon learn how I e-mail. It's rarely more than one line. Often, just a word or two. "Sounds good." "Doubtful." "Great—you nailed it!" "Rework first paragraph, all else stays." "Too much." Ninety percent of the time, that's all it needs. Any more would be wasted time. And if you're e-mailing me, keep it to one topic; if you address more than one thing, you'll probably get a reply to only the first thing you asked.

I have a virtual assistant, Angie, who books all my phone calls and appointments and helps me stay on purpose. "Purpose" is a powerful word; it comes from an Old French word, *purpos*, meaning aim or intention. To be "on purpose" is "to aim accurately." That sounds like a Spec Ops sniper to me. It also sounds like a successful businessperson. With every meeting, every e-mail, every phone call, I have a question going in the back of my mind: "Is there purpose to this conversation? Do I want to build a relationship with this person or this company? Is there purpose behind this meeting that aligns with my life and business strategy?"

If the answer is no, then I pass, every time.

Since I started putting this discipline into practice, my business revenue has quintupled. I've also started making new and more powerful relationships, both in my business and in my life. To the uninitiated, some of this may sound brash or mean-spirited. The initiated know better. Successful executives and business owners hold both their time and their relationships in an iron vault, precious and inviolable.

Know Your Number

When I started my business, I wanted to do three things.

Number one, I wanted to change the world.

If you say that sounds grandiose, I would ask, don't you want the same thing? Why would you even dream of going through the grief and hardship, struggle and stress, of being in business if you *weren't* intending to change the world? I know my business isn't going to feed the world's hungry, or raise global literacy rates, or vaccinate kids in Africa. But do I want to make my mark on the world? Of course I do. I want to leave behind tangible proof that the world is a better place because I was here. Don't you? Doesn't every entrepreneur and hard-charging executive?

At the very least, all ambitious businesspeople *start out* with that impulse. Maybe it gets lost in a long series of setbacks and compromises. People give up on their real dreams and settle for superficial goals. But I believe that, deep down, every person who goes into business wants to change the world for the better, at least in some way.

So that's number one.

Number two, I wanted to serve my community. By "my community," I meant the Special Operations world, both active duty and vets. Although before long (as we'll see in chapter 4), that definition got a good deal broader. But even then, the mission has always remained the same: serve our community with information and perspective, straight and honest, that they aren't getting anywhere else.

Change the world and serve the larger community: call those the big reasons.

And then there was a personal reason. I wanted to hit a number.

Years ago, not long after I left the service, I went through a two-year business program, in the course of which we did an exercise where we had to write down a number that answered the question "What do you need to live your ideal lifestyle?"

We weren't talking here about living on a yacht or buying an island. But I wanted a decent place, and a second home somewhere nice, to be able to eat out X number of times per week, a housekeeper so my place wouldn't be a mess. The ability to handle emergencies without freaking out. My life handled. When I did the math, that came in at right about $400,000 a year.

There were about a hundred of us in this class, all doing the same exercise. Yet even with all the differences in our individual histories and circumstances, we all arrived at right around that same figure.

The next question was, "What does it take to have $400,000 coming in every year, in passive income, so you don't have to keep your nose to the grindstone every week for the rest of your life just to keep things glued together?" The answer, with a give-or-take factor depending on current interest rates, was about $10 million, banked (or, better, invested).

That was my number. That *is* my number. Ten million. (You can see why the Scout Media offer was tempting.)

Maybe you're saying, "Well, I could get by just fine on half of that." Fair enough. Say you need $200,000 a year, so about $16K a month. That's $5 million, banked and/or invested, to produce that much in annual passive income. Which means if you say it would take about $200K to live on, not outrageously but comfortably, with not only day-to-day costs but also vacations and travels and emergencies and other unexpecteds all handled just fine, then what you're saying is, your number is $5 million.

Are you worth $5 million, right now, today? I sure as hell wasn't.

When I did that exercise, it scared the crap out of me. Because I didn't have anywhere near that much. I didn't have any immediate prospects of having anywhere near that much. That fact was, I'd never even identified what that number was, let alone worked out a strategy for how to get there. I'd never sat down and quantified exactly what it was I was shooting for.

Imagine you're in a sniper course and your instructor tells you, "Okay, get ready to shoot, you need to hit this target." *Okay,* you go. *What target? Where is it?* "Oh, we don't know," he says. "We just know there's a target somewhere out there. Go ahead. Start shooting. Maybe you'll find it by hitting it."

It doesn't work that way.

As snipers, we learned a huge amount of the intricate math and physics involved in ballistics. But here's something we learned that isn't intricate at all: if you're not looking at the target, if you don't even know where the target is, then your chances of hitting it are pretty slim.

You have to know your number. If you don't, then there's no point in pulling the trigger, because you have no idea where you're aiming. And once you know your number, you have to develop a business strategy that will produce that kind of asset and therefore that kind of income.

I'm not saying your number should be the same as mine. It might be half that. It might be twice that. It might be something else altogether. It's whatever it is. But you need to *know* what it is, or there's no point being in business.

So what's your number? If you don't know it, you'll never hit it.

Get Clear About Money

Since the subject has come up, let's talk about money.

When you pour all your concentration into that red circle, that central focal point at the front of your scope, is money what you see there? It better be—but it also better *not* be. Because there are three things you need to know about money to succeed in business, and here are the first two:

1. It's about the money.
2. It's not about the money.

I know. Two completely contradictory statements, and they're both true, and you need to be able to hold on to both of them with clarity.

A friend of mine, Kamal Ravikant, has spent years working in the venture capital world and has seen a lot of billion-dollar business ideas. He says, "If you start a business selling spoons because you think spoons are hot right now, everyone's buying spoons, and you can make a killing in spoons, I'm not interested in investing, because I'm pretty sure you'll fail. If you want to start a business in spoons because all your life you've loved spoons, you can't stop thinking about them, you've come up with a hundred ways of designing new and different and cool spoons . . . let's talk."

His point: money, on its own, is not a compelling goal. It's not enough to keep you in the game when the tough challenges come. Money is critical, and you have to know your number. But it's not the oxygen your business burns to stay alive. What is? Your passion. The thing you care about. (We'll hear more from Kamal in chapter 5, "Embrace the Suck.")

So get clear about this: Money is critical. But it can never be the deciding factor. Never make an important business decision based purely on comparative numbers. There are always deeper and more important factors involved.

Which brings us to the third thing you need to know about money to succeed in business:

3. Whatever attitudes, assumptions, beliefs, and opinions you have about money, you need to drop them. Lose them. Right here, right now.

People who have issues around money are the first to say, "Money isn't everything." What they really mean is, "I have a problem with money, so I'm going to pretend it's not really very important." Which is complete bullshit.

The other day, I had a conversation with a friend who's working like crazy in his business, having his struggles. "Yeah," he said, "I just want to do this so I can grow the business and take care of my family."

I asked him, "So how much *is* that, to take care of your family?"

He couldn't answer that. He didn't know his number. Didn't have a clue. So what did he say? "Well, money isn't everything."

I shook my head and said, "Hang on a second. What you just said makes absolutely no sense. There is an actual number that takes care of your mom, your dad, your sisters, your brothers, everyone. But you're afraid to dig it out. No, money isn't everything, but money takes care of the people you want to take care of. It feeds them, it buys health care, it creates experiences.

"Dude," I said, "the reason I know my number is that I have exactly the same concerns you do. I want to take care of my kids and make sure they go to college and they don't have to graduate with a bunch of debt. I want to make sure that if, God forbid, they get hurt, they're taken good care of. I want to be able to spend time with them—a *lot* of time—doing amazing things that they'll remember for the rest of their lives."

He could relate to that. But I'm still not sure he's sat down and nailed his number.

Part of what informs my own perspective has to do with my dad's views on money. I wanted to make sure I didn't have the attitude about it that he did.

My father was very entrepreneurial. Working a construction job, he taught himself everything there was to know about building houses, from framing and roofing to plumbing and electrical wiring. Before long, he ran his own construction business. But he also had some major setbacks and lost his company, and I think that burned him to the point that he didn't trust the world, which made him fearful and stingy with money. One year I really wanted a skateboard, and my mom bought me one at Target. My dad was so pissed at her that he drove off, left her standing there in the parking lot.

I have to admit there was some good modeling there, in that we learned to be careful with our money and not to spend it on frivolous things. But a fearful, overcautious attitude about money can lead you to make bad decisions in business. It can also cripple your ability to live life to the fullest.

My attitude with my kids is, if it's important, if it's valuable, if it enriches their lives, I do it. And if it costs money, so what. I can always make more money. I can't make more time.

Over the past decade, I've seen my dad loosen up a little about money, but the old attitudes die hard. Recently, I wanted to take him to the Stanley Cup finals in Pittsburgh for his birthday. He's a massive hockey fan and a great player himself, but he'd never been to a Stanley Cup play-off game. I bought the tickets; they were trading on Ticketmaster for as much as $2,500, but a pro player friend got them for me at face value, $600 or $700 apiece. I told my dad I'd scored the tickets, and he should book his flight out east.

He said, "Well, I don't know . . . the flight's going to cost a lot. It's too much."

I knew he had the money. I knew he could afford it. But I wasn't about to challenge him. I called Angie and said, "You know what, let's just book his flight and hotel room."

When he found out I'd bought his plane ticket, I could tell he was happy about it—but a part of him was going, *Whoa, why would you do that? That's crazy!*

But it's not crazy, not at all. Being able to have that time with my dad, to share that experience together? That's priceless. He won't be here forever. Hell, none of us will. If I don't use the money for something like this, then what's the point of making it?

My son Hunter recently broke his arm. I took him to the best ortho guy in Tahoe. It cost me three grand. Was it worth it? Are you serious?

People who don't have money suffer for it. They eat cheap processed food and get heart disease and cancer at higher rates. They don't take care of themselves, because they can't afford to. They have more stress in their lives because they're so freaking stretched. They can't afford the best, and it hurts. It's just the facticity of life.

The extremely successful people I know aren't greedy, or selfish, or materialistic. They don't have distorted values. If anything, the opposite. They are the most generous, kind, devoted, caring, clearheaded people I know. All that crap about rich people being egocentric, or corrupt, or uncaring, is complete and total nonsense, concocted to help people who *don't* have money feel more virtuous and better about their lives. Are there unhappy rich people? Sure; I've met some. But I know a lot more people who have built their wealth *and* their happiness, because they found their purpose in life and are passionately focused on what they do, from their businesses to their hobbies, whether it's flying, sailing, or collecting art.

Is business all about the money? Of course not. It's about innovation and ingenuity, about coming up with new and better ways of doing things. It's about making people's lives better. Exercising the incredible creativity of the human spirit. *And* it's about hitting your number: giving you what you need so you can design the life you want and take care of the people you care about.

Making the world a better place, and making *your* world a better place. Two equally noble pursuits. It's not either/or. It's *and*.

So whatever hang-ups you have about money, you need to wipe them away. Get really clear on money.

Keep Your Balance

Earlier I talked about embracing a "healthy state of obsession." Before closing this chapter, I want to put that in perspective. Because total focus is not the same thing as tunnel vision, where you are literally unaware of everything outside your field of attention. That's not focus; that's being an ostrich with your head in the sand. Otherwise known as blissful denial.

In business, also known as suicide.

You have to stay aware of it all *and* at the same time be totally focused. Like most truths that really matter, it's a paradox.

Front sight focus is also not the same thing as being a workaholic. As a sniper, you can't keep performing with consistent accuracy on the gun if you neglect your physical fitness or let your health go to seed. Yes, for those minutes or hours when you're lying prone and drilling your eyesight on a target a thousand yards off, your body becomes a nonexistent irrelevancy—but the only reason you can perform like that is that you've been taking care of it day in and day out. (We'll talk more about your health and fitness in chapter 4.)

The same holds true for your business and the rest of your life outside your business.

The only way you can successfully and consistently focus on your business is if you maintain your health, your family, your relationships, and all the rest of what makes you a human being in a healthy state of balance. There's a point where work takes precedence, and whenever that point comes, you know you simply have to lock the doors and rivet yourself on getting the job done. And there's a time when you have to shift your attention to your family, your kids, your girlfriend or boyfriend, your circle of friends.

If you see those things as taking away from your business, then you're not looking at it right. Those things aren't detracting *from* your business. They are what allows you to be successful *in* your business.

A few years ago, *Men's Journal* wrote a profile on me that included this day-in-the-life excerpt from my Facebook page:

> My last 30 hours: 0400 Uber to JFK, 0600 nonstop to LAX, CBS studios, lunch with Mark Harmon (great guy), kids call, CNN call, dinner with friends and agent Valarie, friend Sally drops me at LAX, miss flight, standby for 1130 to JFK, coach seat secured, flt crew upgrades me to 1st class sleeper, 0730 land, 0830 NYAC [New York Athletic Club] swim 2,000 meters. Start my Saturday.

This is pretty typical for me. Am I busy? I am.

At the same time, as I write these words, I just finished a week unplugged and off the map with my three kids, somewhere in the Northwest, having a blast with them. Total dad time. It's one of those things that gives my life depth and meaning. Without it, I'd be a pale copy of myself. I made a pledge to myself years ago, when my first business fell apart and my wife and I divorced, that I would never let business get in the way of spending time with my kids. As I wrote in

The Red Circle, "The marriage may not have made it, but the family is forever. That, too, is part of my red circle."

You have those things, too, that make you who you are. You know what they are. You have to keep them in your red circle, too.

It's a matter of balance, and balance is a matter of doing one thing at a time—and being very, very clear on exactly what that one thing is.

PROFILE: JOE APFELBAUM
(AJAX UNION)

As I said in the introduction, I have a circle of friends I look to for insight and inspiration—and, in those times when I need it, for guidance. They are all super-successful. I call them my "Spec Ops friends of the business world." No one better exemplifies the principle of front sight focus than Joe Apfelbaum, CEO of the Brooklyn-based digital marketing company Ajax Union.

As successful as Joe is, it took some bitter failure and heartbreak to get him there.

Joe grew up in an Orthodox Jewish community where, when you get married, it's very important to have kids right away. In 2003, all of Joe's married friends were having kids, but not Joe and his new bride. People who knew them started talking: Why weren't the Apfelbaums having kids? After a year of this, Joe and his wife started seeing doctors, going through tests, and doing all kinds of research. It became a huge source of stress in Joe's life.

Finally, they got pregnant. They were so excited they had a celebration at his mother's house and another at his wife's mother's house. Everybody they knew was happy for them. They told the whole world.

A few weeks before their due date, Joe was at his office when he got a call from his wife, who was crying so hard he could barely understand her. She was at the hospital for a routine test. The doctors said they couldn't find a heartbeat.

"They don't know what they're talking about," said Joe. "I'll be there in a few minutes."

One of Joe's strengths is that he has an amazing ability to become an expert at pretty much anything he turns his mind to. (His mother used to call him Touchy-Touch when he was little, because he would go around touching and messing with everything until he became an expert at it.) By this time, he was running a few different businesses and had already acquired a reputation as a master troubleshooter. As far as he was concerned, there wasn't a problem that couldn't be fixed.

He would just go over to that hospital and fix this one.

He walked in, full of confidence, and when the attendant said, "Mr. Apfelbaum, I'm so sorry for your loss," Joe replied, "What loss? There's no loss here. Let me speak to the doctor. Bring me the head cardiologist."

For two days, Joe battled to make it not true. Finally, he had to accept that he and his wife had lost their baby.

A deep sadness settled over Joe, like a black cloud. "This was my purpose for being here," he says. "This was the reason I came to this world. And now I'd failed. It felt like my life was over." He sent his employees home and closed his businesses—maybe permanently. He wasn't really sure. He wasn't sure of anything.

After a few weeks, someone called to offer him a job. Joe didn't want to take it—like most entrepreneurs, he considered himself unemployable—but the guy pressed. He'd just sold a $100,000 piece of software to somebody in Minnesota who was having trouble with it, and Joe was the only person he knew who could figure things like this out on the fly. He needed Joe to get out to Minnesota and figure the damn thing out.

Joe asked his wife what she thought.

"Look," she said. "For the past two weeks you've been sitting around the house, moping and crying, driving me crazy. I can't take it. You need to go do this, or we're getting divorced."

Joe agreed to take the job if his new employer would let him run his other businesses on the side, and the guy said yes. He spent a little phone time with the software company's staff, read a few books on the subject, flew out to Minnesota, and within three or four hours of messing with it, he had the problem solved.

Okay. So he hadn't fathered a child. But he could do *this*.

Joe poured himself into his work again. At his new job, he became an expert at IT. Every time Google changed its algorithm, Joe would reverse-engineer it and figure out what he needed to do to get his clients to the top. It was like a game for Joe—a game that paid *very* well. He started an IT consulting business on the side. He became an expert at selling things on the Internet. He became an expert at Web site construction, graphic design, marketing. He read entire shelves of books, about everything and anything. He worked until three in the morning every day.

During the next few years, he went through a series of four full-time jobs, all while running seven businesses on the side, in an office with eight full-time employees. He had a construction company building sukkahs (ceremonial huts used for Sukkot) with three crews building units each year for four hundred customers. He ran a real estate Web site. An SEO (search engine optimization) company. A graphic design business. An eBay business. He was doing a million things and executing flawlessly. But deep down, he knew it was crazy.

"I said *yes* to everything," says Joe. "But I knew I was doing something wrong. It's just not humanly possible for someone to do all that and be successful at all of it."

Joe had grown up working after school and on weekends in his mother's clothing shop on Manhattan's Lower East Side. He had seen her go from selling sweaters to flying all over the world to buy the best fabrics and selling high-end couture under her own label at half the department stores' prices. She was successful, to a point—but she could never break the million-dollar mark. Joe had watched her business struggle for more than a decade before finally going under.

Now something weirdly similar was happening to him. He wasn't *failing* . . . but something was keeping him from being as successful as he should be. The truth was, he was a mile wide and an inch deep.

In 2008, a business partner, Zevi Friedman, approached Joe about starting an online marketing company. Joe said yes (of course), and the two started a digital marketing company they named Ajax Union. Joe now had yet one more part-time horse to ride in his jam-packed stable.

At the time, Joe had a full-time position as chief marketing officer for TheWatchery.com, a luxury watch business, where he managed about a hundred people in its sales and marketing division. Even as the Great Recession was killing a lot of other luxury businesses, Joe helped it grow from $3 million to $40 million in a very short time.

In April 2009, after Ajax Union had been going for a while and was showing some serious growth, Joe walked into the office of Watchery's CEO, Joseph Levy, and said, "Joseph, you know I have seven side gigs that I do, right?"

"Yeah, of course," said Levy. "How's that going?"

"It's going well," said Joe. "Actually, this one business in particular is really taking off. We have thirty clients, we're growing, and my partner wants me to come work full-time. But I love you, I love this company, and I love working here. What should I do?"

"Listen," said Levy. "First of all, I want to thank you. Because of you, I've grown my company from $3 million to $40 million, and we'll be selling it soon. You should go build that business. What's more, I want to be your biggest customer."

Joe went back to Zevi and said he was ready to work full-time in their business—and much to his astonishment Zevi said, "No. That's not going to work for me."

"*What?* What are you talking about?" said Joe.

Zevi said, "Joe, you need to focus."

"What do you mean, I need to focus? I'm *incredibly* focused!"

Zevi shook his head. "No, you need to get rid of everything you're doing on the side. Everything. Let go of all of it. You need this to be the *only* thing you're doing."

Joe was shocked. "I can't do that! I'm making so much money from my sukkah business, and my eBay business, and my advertising platform, and . . ."

Zevi looked at him and said, "Joe. We can build a multimillion-dollar company here. But we're not going to do that if you're doing all this other stuff. I need you to *focus*."

Joe was stunned.

He went and talked to his wife. She said, "Do it. If it means we take a financial hit, that's okay, you'll make up for it with Ajax Union. You'll figure it out."

Joe took a deep breath and made the plunge. He sold the sukkah business; closed down his eBay business; shuttered his IT company, handing its client list off to a few other IT companies he knew; pulled the plug on a bunch of Web sites; and folded the resources of his Web design and online marketing businesses into Ajax Union. He got rid of *everything*. It was like reaching into his pockets, turning them inside out, and giving everything away—like jumping off the highest high dive without knowing for sure how much water was in the pool.

In the process, Joe says, Zevi helped him realize something. He'd never really been excited about all those different businesses; what he'd been excited about was *promoting* them. Joe had a passion for promoting things—ideas, concepts, values, businesses. Focusing all his energies into a single digital marketing business allowed him to tap into that passion.

Ajax Union took off. Eighteen months after Joe went full-time, the company hit No. 178 on the *Inc.* 500, an annual list of the fastest-growing private companies in America. In 2010, it doubled its revenue, from $500,000 to $1 million, and then doubled it again the following year to over $2 million. By 2015, the revenue was $4 million, and as of this writing the company's on track for $6 million in 2016.

Joe has also become an expert in a whole new topic: focus.

"Most people don't really know what they want," he says. "If you don't know where you want to go, you might end up getting some-where else. Where? I don't know. But it's probably not somewhere you'll be happy with."

Like me, Joe is big on the word "purpose."

"If you know what you want to do and focus intensely on that purpose, you'll move forward—but you have to put all your chips into one basket and go all in. If you don't do that, you'll die."

Joe says focus is a skill, and as with any skill, to become good at it you need to practice it. Not just the kind of hyper-focusing you do when it's suddenly crunch time, but focusing each and every day on whatever is the most important thing, on that particular day, toward reaching your goal.

He has also brought that dedication to focus to how he works with his clients. He doesn't just help them market their business; he also coaches them to help them get clear on exactly what that business is at its core.

"Most businesses fail in the first year," he tells them, "and most of those still standing fail within the first three. Very few get past five. Almost none get past ten. And you know what most of those failures have to do with? Lack of focus."

Today Joe is one of the most focused guys I know. He's also one of the happiest.

And by the way, he and his wife now have five beautiful children.

You're probably wondering what happened after that lunch with Todd Dakarmen, when he called me on my lack of focus.

A week later I got another phone call. "Hi, Brandon? Todd Dakarmen. Look, I want to set up our next shooting date." He was a man who knew what he wanted, all right.

But now so was I. "Sorry, man," I told him. "I can't do it. I've taken your advice. I'm focusing."

He laughed. "Son of a bitch!" he said. "Good for you."

I made that call staring off the La Jolla coast and let go of Wind Zero. Unlike Todd's crashed Porsches, the thing was not salvageable, not even for parts. Four million dollars' worth of investor money and my life savings, gone. Chalk that up to one expensive postgraduate course in business. I took a position with a large defense firm in

San Diego, just to have something to pay the bills and consolidate my finances while I figured out what the hell to do next. Over the rest of that year, I let go of a bunch of other projects I was working on and gave a pass to a lot of strong opportunities I'd been considering. I got laser focused. I needed to find that single target.

Within a few months, I did.

I scraped together about $10,000 and in February 2012 launched a Web site, SOFREP.com, which stood for "Special Operations Forces Situation Report" (like the military term "SITREP," for "situation report"). That became my front sight focus.

By the end of the year, we had more than a million people hitting the site each month. Our weekly SOFREP Radio broadcast became the No. 1 broadcast in its category on iTunes. We had a publishing division going that would generate several *New York Times* bestsellers. Over the next few years, we launched or acquired more than half a dozen related Web sites, including SpecialOperations.com and the gear site Loadout Room, and I formed an umbrella entity, Hurricane Group, Inc., to bring all these properties together into one unified digital media empire. In 2014, a media company offered to buy it all from me for $15 million, and you already know where that went. A year later, Hurricane was worth triple that, and today it's worth a good deal more. There have been other offers. I'm still not selling.

It's amazing what can happen in a few short years. All the success that had failed to materialize with Wind Zero happened with SOFREP and Hurricane. And I trace it all back to that conversation with Todd.

Over these last few years, I've said no to a lot of strong opportunities, some of them truly amazing situations. It still happens today. On average, I say no to a solid business offer about once a week.

"Will you consult for my company? Will you join this board of directors? Are you interested in being my partner investor?" Sorry—no can do. I'm focused on my target.

You're also probably wondering how that B-52 bomb drop worked out.

I called the numbers, and seconds later the bomb fell—about a hundred yards behind the fighters who were shooting at us. I made a quick recalculation and called up new numbers. The second drop was right on target. We're still here. The other guys aren't.

Sometimes that's the only outcome that counts.

Chapter 2

TOTAL SITUATIONAL
AWARENESS

❖ ● ❖

As the high-speed train sped through the French country-side on its way to Paris late in the day on August 21, 2015, a man slipped out of the bathroom to make his way back into the crowded passenger car. His mission was simple: kill as many people as possible, and he was well equipped to deliver on that promise. With an AKM assault rifle slung over one shoulder and plenty of ammunition, plus a loaded handgun and box cutter as side weapons, he was fully armed and ready to deliver another massacre on European soil in the name of jihad.

Except that it didn't work out that way.

Two Frenchmen who happened to be nearby and saw the guy emerge from the restroom tried unsuccessfully to subdue him. At which point a group of three American friends—two of them off-duty military men—launched a split-second counterattack. Spencer Stone (air force) slowed the assailant down by grappling with him, sustaining multiple slash wounds as he struggled to get him into a choke hold. Alek Skarlatos (national guard) grabbed the rifle away from the guy and slammed the muzzle into his head, immobilizing him. Their friend Anthony Sadler helped hold him down and tie him up with another passenger's T-shirt.

There was a lot of blood and a lot of panic—but nobody died.

Nobody died. Think about that for a moment. In these days of mass shooters and rampant acts of terrorism, a jihadist armed with an automatic rifle and nine magazines totaling 270 rounds launches himself into a crowded train carrying more than five hundred passengers, intent on unleashing a massacre—and fails to kill a single person.

Here's what I find remarkable about this. Stone and Skarlatos were not there on patrol or acting as security forces. They were not there in any official capacity, and they certainly weren't focusing on this guy. They were on vacation. They were focusing on fun and sightseeing. (Hell, Stone was *sleeping* when the attack began.) There is one and only one reason this situation didn't become the tragic bloodbath that it so easily could have been: these guys had a particular kind of training.

They were trained to be *situationally aware.*

One year after that foiled train attack, almost to the day, I landed at JFK after a few weeks in Europe. I had just cleared customs and was waiting for my luggage when I heard a scuffle of people running and half a dozen officers burst into the area shouting, "Shots fired! Active shooter! Everyone run for safety—RUN!"

I immediately took cover behind a concrete pillar (*concealment* is something that hides you visually but can still be penetrated by gunfire; *cover* is something that protects you both visually and ballistically) and began assessing the scene. I saw a mother running for her life with a baby in her arms. A man crying because he was separated from his wife and children. Hundreds of people pouring through alarm-wired security doors searching for safety. Nobody had any idea what was happening. No police or TSA agents or security personnel showed up to tell everyone what to do. Pandemonium. The noise level was insane. It felt as if I were back in Afghanistan or Iraq in the middle of some op—only nobody'd been briefed.

Leapfrogging backward, using whatever points of cover presented themselves, I found an exit that was open. Another wave of panicked people was headed my way. Someone had to take charge, so I shouted, "Follow me!" and out we went, down the stairs, out onto the tarmac, and to a fence that separated the airport grounds from a parking lot. Throwing my rain jacket over the top of the razor-wire to create a passable avenue of escape, I helped a few people over and out. Some officers saw us and were not happy with me. But *someone* had to have a plan. The place was such total chaos it's a miracle nobody was trampled to death by the stampeding herds of terrified passengers.

As it turned out, there was no shooter. The whole thing was a case of panic over nothing. Someone put forward the theory that the sound of people cheering on the televised Olympics was somehow mistaken for gunfire. Sounds like a bullshit rumor to me, something someone concocted to cover his ass. Way more likely is that it was an accidental gun discharge. But whatever it was that triggered the panic isn't the point.

The point is this: *Nobody* was prepared. *Nobody* was situationally aware.

In the wake of mass-shooting incidents around the world, many of us from the Spec Ops community have been called upon to help train citizens on what to do in the event of a sudden shooting rampage or other unexpected attack. We've written about it over and over on

SOFREP. Of all the advice and perspective I can possibly offer, the single most critical element in safety, prevention, and defense is the combination of skills summed up in the three words at the top of this chapter.

Total situational awareness.

You need the same skill set to survive and thrive in the world of business.

Plan, Look, Listen

When I was a kid, there was a railroad crossing not far from my house that sported an old wooden sign with three words on it. You've probably seen one like it. It said, STOP • LOOK • LISTEN. That's a great piece of life advice, too. But it doesn't quite work on the battlefield, because when trouble hits like a hurricane, there isn't time to STOP and think. The LOOK and LISTEN part is spot-on, but if you have to STOP first to do it, then you're already too late—and someone's dead. Maybe you.

You have to do the thinking ahead of time. You have to PLAN.

Total situational awareness is what you achieve when you practice *forethought and thorough preparation,* combined with a state of *moderate vigilance.*

The forethought and preparation aspect means that by the time you're in the situation, you've already asked questions like "What would I do if *XYZ* happened, or something like it?" You've visualized unexpected problems, run scenarios, created contingencies. You can't anticipate everything that could go wrong, but you can anticipate enough so that you at least have a plan of action, or the bare bones of a plan of action, for when the shit hits the fan.

At JFK, nobody had a plan. And the guys on the train? They didn't have to STOP to come up with a plan, because they had training. They'd run scenarios. Not exactly like this situation, but close enough that they could move right into action. If they'd had to STOP and think about it, there would have been dozens of fatalities on that train, probably starting with them.

Then there's the moderate vigilance part. This isn't the same thing as being *hypervigilant*, that all-nerves-tingling state you go to in the midst of an actual emergency, where adrenaline floods your system, your senses become acute, and time slows down to a crawl. If you maintained that kind of vigilance for any length of time, you'd go nuts. Or suffer adrenal exhaustion. Or both. Moderate vigilance means that even as you go about your business, a part of you stays on *mild* alert, tuning in to what's going on around you.

Americans by nature tend to be among the least situationally aware people on the planet. When I walk the streets of New York, it amazes me how many people stroll along glued to their phones, barely seeing where they're going themselves, let alone noticing what other people are doing or how they are acting. These blissful unawares don't have a clue who is in the crowd around them. If an active-shooter situation suddenly broke out, they would be completely lost.

Total situational awareness means you never let yourself get too comfortable. The truth is, most of us in the modern developed world live very sheltered lives. For a lot of people, most of the time, maybe that works.

In business, it's sure death.

Pay Attention

Let's try something. Think about the last time you went shopping. Not online, I mean the last time you actually walked into a physical store. Drugstore, convenience store, supermarket, whatever. Got that clearly in mind? Okay.

Now take a piece of paper, and write down a list of every single person you saw while you were in that store, describing each person's face, manner of movement, and your overall impression.

How'd you do?

If the police knocked on your door tomorrow, sat down in your living room, said they were investigating a recent crime in the area, and asked you if any of the people you passed in the store when you were there had acted oddly in any way, how much information could you give them? How useful a witness would you be?

In sniper training, we have an exercise we call KIM, or Keep in Memory. There are dozens of variations. In one, instructors might drive you through the streets of a city to a destination and, after you get there, quiz you without warning on every car you passed along the way. In another, you go through a field course where objects are hidden out in the woods along the way. You're supposed to remember them all, which means that you have to have noticed them all, even though nobody told you that you'd be tested on this later. Those students *always* had to be "on." Always vigilant. Sometimes, to push the limits of our students' memories, we would wait a few weeks after they'd been through a given course to quiz them on what they saw there.

The point of these exercises is to train our students in how to pay extreme attention and cultivate total situational awareness.

It surprises most people to learn this, but being a sniper is not principally about shooting or marksmanship. As a sniper, a relatively tiny percentage of your total amount of time in the field is on the gun. You spend most of your active time in *observation*. A sniper is first and foremost an intelligence asset. Snipers are a field element's forward eyes and ears. Reconnaissance and surveillance are the bedrock of our skill set.

The same is true in business. Do you make important decisions? Of course. Do you pull the trigger—hiring and firing, writing checks, launching initiatives? Of course you do. But not most of the time. No, the great majority of what you're called upon to do is learn, watch, absorb, think. Reconnaissance. Paying attention.

Those three weeks I was in Europe, just before finding myself in the middle of that phantom-shooter incident at JFK? I called it a vacation, but that isn't really what it was. To be fair, I did a bunch of sightseeing, saw friends, flew some planes. I'm a big believer in the "work hard, play hard" philosophy. But the real purpose of that trip was to do some fact-finding. I wanted to get a firsthand read on what was happening with the economy in Europe, how our own forthcoming presidential election might affect markets over there, and what was going on globally. While I was there, I met with people whom friends from home had hooked me up with—entrepreneurs from Berlin, Australia, Russia, all over. Reconnaissance. Paying attention.

I consume a steady diet of industry periodicals for the media business and read a ton of books (which I'll say more about in a moment), but it's not enough to read what's on the page or the screen. You have to be constantly reading the world around you.

Next time you're out walking around in public, ask yourself, if someone suddenly mounted an armed attack, where would it most likely come from? What would be your best escape route?

Now ask those same questions about your business.

Practice Using Your Peripheral Vision

As I said, an expert military sniper is not simply an expert marksman but a highly skilled observer. Therefore, a significant part of sniper training has to do with how to *see*. For example, in sniper school you learn that looking directly at something is not necessarily the best way to see it. Sometimes your peripheral vision serves you better than your dead-on-target focal vision.

Detecting color and movement are the two most important factors in observation. The central area of the retina, called the fovea, is not very good at seeing those. The fovea is excellent at detail in black-and-white, which is what you pick up when you scan a page of text with the center of your eyes: the black-and-white details of letters and words. Peripheral vision, on the other hand, is lousy at detail but far more acute at picking up color and movement. Terrible at reading static words on the page, but superb at noticing something—or someone—moving out in the woods at the edge of your field of vision.

Try this: Hold your hand out straight and make a thumbs-up gesture. Now look at your thumbnail. That covers about 2 percent of your field of vision, the total area that your foveal receptors encompass. That tiny hole in the center of your field of vision is the detail peephole you use to scan back and forth on a page when you read. It also represents the scope of your brain when it's trying to bear down on a problem by focusing. Lots of detail. Hardly any depth or context. No color.

Now, as you continue staring at your thumbnail, don't move your eyes or change your focus, but just become aware of everything in your field of vision *other* than your thumbnail. The first thing you'll notice is how much more there is to see! That's a vast ocean of visible information—none of which you can access, or at least not very well, when you try to focus on it.

Focus, in other words, isn't everything, as important as it is. That's the paradox of the sniper's craft: you have to be totally focused on your target *as if* you were shutting out the rest of the world—but you're not shutting it out. In fact you have to be keenly tuned in to what's going on in the rest of the world.

Business is like that, too. You can't live in a silo. And it's not only danger that may come at you from the periphery; it's also opportunity. Whether you're a small-business owner, entrepreneur, solo practitioner, or department manager for a monster firm, you can't afford to say, "Oh, I don't need to know about that business over there; it's got nothing to do with what *we* do here." Because today it might not, but you never know if tomorrow it suddenly will.

Blockbuster video didn't think the online digital world had anything to do with its business model, any more than the big-box bookstore chains did before Amazon came along. You can't afford to bury your head in your own sandbox. You never know when something in the periphery will assume central importance.

In 2011, when I was licking my wounds from the Wind Zero

meltdown, there were two proven paths where a guy with my background could go to work and make serious money: consulting to defense companies, and farming himself out overseas as a contract security agent. I'd done both, and I wasn't interested in making either one my future. There were also lucrative executive opportunities in the corporate sector. Did that too; also not my future.

But . . . blogging? I mean, seriously? The idea that someone like me could build a multimillion-dollar media empire starting with a blog site was so out in left field it would have been easy to miss completely.

But there you go: "out in left field" is the very definition of peripheral vision.

Sometimes, while you're busy taking aim at the target directly in front of you, there's a much better idea floating at the periphery of your vision, something you hadn't thought of and never would have in a million years. And if you keep your eyes staring straight ahead to the exclusion of all else, you'll miss it.

Stay Thirsty

On February 1, 2012, we put up our first few posts on SOFREP.

On February 2, I wrote a post saying, "Thank you for checking out the site and all the great feedback yesterday. We're still working out some bugs, and I'm tracking all your inputs to make sure we have the best site possible. As we say in the navy, welcome aboard— and please help us spread the world about SOFREP! Brandon out."

My brand-new business had now been up and online for twenty-four hours. It was official: I was now the CEO of a media business.

Wait. A *media* business? What the hell did I know about media?

In the course of my SEAL sniper training, I'd gone through a ton of study: not only self-defense and all the obvious combat arts, but also math, physics, ballistics, digital communications, intelligence, history, psychology . . . the list went on and on. To become a SEAL sniper instructor and course master, I pushed my studies even further: education theory, curriculum design, and more. While in the service, I'd dabbled in real estate, so I'd pursued some self-taught business training, too. And the years working on Wind Zero had been a crash course in investment finance, commercial real estate law, and a lot more besides.

But advertising? Media? Sure, in the past year I'd taught myself a bit about digital media while helping build up a site for the company I blogged for part-time. Still, I was certainly no expert.

I knew I damn well better become one, though, and fast.

Yes, SOFREP was essentially a blog, and we were in business to provide good readable content. But the business itself was about a lot more than writing content. The economic lifeblood of the business was advertising. I needed to understand how advertising worked, both so I could speak our potential clients' language and so we could help make sure they got results on our site. And I needed to understand how marketing and media worked so I could manage the effort to drive more readers to our site, because the value your Web site offers to your advertisers (and thus how much you can charge them) depends directly on the volume of your traffic.

It was really three businesses rolled into one: generating content, driving traffic, building advertisers.

Which is not atypical, because no business is a solitary thing. All businesses are inherently complex and multifaceted. Being a business owner is a lot like being a Special Operator in the field: you may not be the designated sniper, or breacher, or intelligence guy, or comms operator, but you sure as hell better know your way around any and all of those disciplines, and more. You have to be prepared to be anything and everything. I might not have been a marketing guy when I started SOFREP—but now I *had* to be a marketing guy, and I had to be one *now*.

I threw myself into the study of marketing, advertising, and media. I read voraciously, all the best books on those topics I could find. I started chowing down three, four, six, a dozen books a week. Five years later, I'm still doing it. About once a week, when I'm in New York, I go down to Alabaster Bookshop near Union Square and say, "Okay, what have you got for me?" They know what I like, and whenever I show up, they have a stack of books waiting for me that they've picked out, the best reads on advertising, marketing, and design, from the 1950s through today. At this point, I've read just about all of them, at least the titles that matter.

Right now, as I write this, I'm looking up from my desk in my little place in New York City and looking over at a stack of books I've read (or reread) in the past few months. From the floor up, the stack stands almost as tall as I am.

Mid-Century Ads

The Art of Thinking Clearly

Contagious: Why Things Catch On

Milton Friedman's *Free to Choose*

The Next Convergence

The *All-American Ads* books

The Best American Infographics

Ogilvy on Advertising, probably the best of them all. I've been very strongly influenced by Ogilvy; we have his famous quotation on advertising emblazoned on our Hurricane Web site: "If it doesn't sell, it's not creative."

Born in 1842: A History of Advertising

A History of Graphic Design

100 Ideas That Changed Advertising

Understanding Media, Culture Is Our Business, and all the rest of Marshall McLuhan's stuff

Reality in Advertising, by Rosser Reeves, one of the best out of all I've read

Bill Bernbach's Book; Bernbach was the guy who created "We Try Harder" for Avis, "Think Small" for VW, and the kid Mikey for Life cereal; brilliant guy.

How to Win Friends and Influence People, Dale Carnegie, an old standby, and still one of the most valuable business books I've ever read

I'm skipping over some titles; there's a bunch of military, economics, and general history in there, too. Because I run a media business, the majority of what I read are books on media and advertising, but I also like to keep absorbing knowledge in a broad swath. You never know what you'll need to know.

People sometimes ask me what kind of training it takes to become a SEAL. But that's not really how it works. How it works is, you train like hell, then become a SEAL, and that's when you really *start* training. SEALs are notorious for this: training, training, always training. The more you sweat in training, the expression goes, the less you bleed in battle. (Which is true, except that SEALs often bleed in training, too.)

That obsession with training has its counterpart in business, which is the constant and relentless quest for knowledge. Become a ravenous observer of everything in your field. Know more than the other guy. Stay thirsty for knowledge and more knowledge, perspective and more perspective, grasp and greater grasp.

Know More Than You Think You Need to Know

I am constantly amazed at how many people I run into in business who seem to think they can succeed by knowing just enough to get the job done. The curse of mediocrity.

Just enough is *never* enough, not even close to enough. In the SEALs, we train to extremes, because conditions on the battlefield will always be worse in some way, tougher in some way, far more difficult in a hundred ways, than you expect. There's a famous expression in the military, coined by the Prussian army chief of staff Helmuth von Moltke, the father of modern military strategy: "No battle plan survives contact with the enemy."

In other words, nothing ever goes according to plan: first rule of combat, first rule of business.

Which means that if you are absolutely and completely prepared for things to go the way you expect, you've already lost. Don't get me wrong: you have to *be* absolutely and completely prepared for things to go the way you expect. But you also have to be ready for them to go sideways, moments after you pull the trigger.

In early 2004, my SEAL Team Three teammate John Zinn (whom I mentioned in chapter 1) and his Green Beret buddy Ron were nearly killed in Iraq when their retrofitted American SUV crapped out on them. Back in the States, the two developed their idea for an armored vehicle manufactured to fit the needs of combat. Partnering with a race car manufacturer, they built a prototype, showed it to potential clients, and soon had a $10 million contract lined up. Everything looked great—until John and Ron learned that their manufacturing partner had gone behind their backs to deal with the client directly and cut John and Ron out of the contract. They immediately sued and won, which was all well and good, but they still had a $10 million contract to fulfill—and no manufacturer to build the vehicles for them!

This is exactly the kind of unplanned circumstance that has put many an entrepreneur out of business. Except John understood the principle of total situational awareness and knew that you have to plan for the unplanned.

John had never expected or intended to become an automaker himself, but because he had read so much, studied so much, paid so much attention to that world, he already knew exactly how to do it, what resources they'd need, what the process looked like, and what it would take to tool up. Which is exactly what he and Ron did.

Overnight, they became a manufacturing company and built the damn things themselves. A few years later, John and Ron sold Indigen Armor to the Defense Venture Group for eight figures.

In business, as on the battlefield, everything is in flux. You cannot count on any conditions to stay stable while you enact your carefully thought-out plans. Because they won't. What worked last week, yesterday, five minutes ago, may not work right now. And there is never time to take a step back and catch up before you act; you have to be aware of what *could* happen before it *does* happen.

Which of course is yet another paradox: you can't know what you don't know, and you can't be fully prepared for the unexpected. But you *can* develop the habit of knowing more than you think you need to know, and that will give you the edge you need to succeed when everyone else falls short.

Learn from the Best

There's a principle in psychology called illusory superiority, also sometimes called the Lake Wobegon effect, from Garrison Keillor's fictional midwestern town where "all the children are above average." Illusory superiority is the weird psychological wrinkle that allows the majority of people to have the sense that they are in some way better than average. Smarter than most, luckier than most, more ethical than most, more deserving than most. Mathematically it makes no sense. How can the majority be better than average? (I think it's related to the idea that violence could never happen here, in *our* neighborhood. Also known as denial.)

I pay attention to the opposite principle, which I think of as the Law of Most. The Law of Most says that by definition most businesses are *not* exceptional. (If they were, the word "exceptional" would be meaningless.) Most marketers, most consultants, most realtors, most lawyers, most writers, most designers, are *not* at the top of their field. It's just how things are. "Top" only means *top* when it stands in distinction to everything else.

This is why you should not believe everything you read. Because the Law of Most applies to experts, too. By definition, most experts are mediocre.

There are experts, and then there are *experts*. Just because someone wrote a book and sold a bunch of copies doesn't mean he is right or that he knows what he's talking about. Among all those books I've read on marketing, I'm sure there isn't one in which I didn't find *something* valuable I could take away from the reading. But I'll go through fifty books before I find one that makes me go, "Okay—*this* guy really has figured it out."

How many books have I read on marketing? Two hundred, maybe three hundred; maybe more. How many do I rely on daily, do I consider my North Star, my 100 percent trusted go-to guides? I can count them on one hand.

This is the reason I eventually formed an advisory board for my business: to surround myself with people who can help me read the world, experts whose experience, knowledge, and judgment I can trust absolutely. But in that first year, I didn't have an advisory board. I barely had advisers, period.

A few months before launching SOFREP, I took out a VA loan and bought a little place in Lake Tahoe, Nevada, so I could get out of the insanely high tax burden of Southern California and start my new business in a no-tax state. It was a good move, but for much of that first year in business I lived like a monk. I worked with my small team and stayed connected to friends I respected and could ask for advice when and if I really needed it. Mostly, though, I was on my own.

Except that I stayed in constant touch with my lawyer, Michael Zinn. This is a guy I knew well and could trust without reservation. Not only was he a decorated Vietnam vet, but he was also the father of my SEAL Team Three teammate John. When I say I would not hesitate to put my life in his hands, that's not a figure of speech. Mike was like an advisory group of one, a mentor and resource I turned to more than once to help me out of a tight spot or make a difficult decision.

In the course of that year, I learned something invaluable: when you find even one person whose expertise and judgment you can absolutely rely upon, you've found something more valuable than all the startup capital in the world. Because that one trusted adviser's perspective contributes significantly to your total situational awareness.

Don't Trust Conventional Wisdom

When my SEAL memoir, *The Red Circle*, was in production, our publisher sent my writing partner and me some sample files it had recorded for the audiobook version, with a voice actor reading the text.

Hang on a sec, I thought. Were audiobook rights part of the contract I'd signed? I didn't think so. I asked our literary agent; she checked; nope. Just an oversight, we were assured. We could do a quick addendum to the contract to sign over the audio rights. No problem.

Wait. Were we sure we wanted to do that? We hadn't actually sold those rights yet. What if we held on to them and produced the audiobook version ourselves?

No, no, no, I was told. You don't want to do that. You don't want that headache! These guys are professionals. They know how to get it done and out into all the retail channels, and besides, they've already recorded the whole thing.

I thought about that. This is how it's done, I get that. But does that mean it's how it *should* be done?

I did some quick research to see roughly what it would cost to pay an audio producer to hire the voice talent, do the studio work, and edit the thing into a final product. I ran some numbers. We'd have to spend a few thousand bucks out of pocket up front, but we would make a hell of a lot more money doing it this way than taking the meager audiobook percentage that is standard in New York publishing contracts.

I talked it over with my writing partner. At first he thought I was crazy to take on the added burden of production, but when I explained the numbers and logistics, he was in. (He's an entrepreneur, too.)

"Tell them sorry but no thanks," I told our agent. "We'll do it ourselves."

I hired an audio producer. As a bonus, I wrote and recorded a special introduction to each chapter, a feature not in any other version of the book. We produced the audio version and marketed it ourselves through Amazon's Audible.com. We made out like bandits. Even today, years later, that self-produced audiobook is a steady stream of decent monthly income for us.

When you hear "This is the way things are done," or "This is the way things are," don't believe it. Conventional wisdom is not always wrong—but it's always suspect. The assumptions and givens most businesspeople operate on are reflections of that telltale adjective, "most." "Most" means average, and average means mediocre, and mediocre is the opposite of what we're talking about here. What we're looking for is *outstanding*.

Know Your Business's Numbers

In chapter 1, I mentioned Wind Zero, the business I worked on for a few years when I first got out of the service.

Wind Zero was an ambitious plan. The place was designed with shooting ranges, tracks for driving instruction, indoor classroom space, lodging and dining facilities for up to two hundred people, plus two helo pads and an airstrip. We would be able to embed actual buildings and cities that we could dress up so we could run large-scale urban-environment exercises, such as riot situations and other high-threat scenarios. We could facade the area out as an Afghan village one week, an urban downtown the next. A lot of California race car clubs were telling us what a market there was for a racing facility, so we added in a full Grand Prix–style double race track where we could hold private sponsored race car events, along with facilities for storing cars in between events. The thing would cost something like $100 million all told. By the end of 2006, I had found my property, a thousand acres of raw land in the Southern California desert. The parcel cost north of $2 million; I plunked down three hundred grand—my total savings—and began working on raising the rest.

When I started work on the project, a friend and fellow former SEAL, Randy Kelley, let me work out of his office space. In those days, I was completely intimidated by business financials. I didn't know how to read a balance sheet or a P&L statement. Not only that, but I really didn't want to know how. As far as I could see, Randy was brilliant at this, so I asked him to help me work up my business plan, which he did. Whenever I had to revise my plan, I would ask Randy to do the numbers for me, which he would generously agree to do.

Finally he said, "Listen, man, you're always asking me to do the numbers, and I'm happy to do it. But you know what? I shouldn't be doing it. *You* need to do it."

"Man," I said, "I really don't want to do the numbers."

He nodded. "Right. And it's because you don't want to do the numbers that you need to do the numbers."

Randy forced me to get over my fear of the unknown and learn the goddamn numbers. The funny thing about it is, today I love doing the numbers. What I discovered is that reading a business financial is not at all complicated. It isn't as if we were doing calculus or advanced trigonometry here. It's just basic arithmetic.

I was talking recently to a friend who's getting out of the military and looking to start a business. "You know," he said, "one of the first things I want to do is hire myself a good CFO. I'm just not a numbers guy."

I had to laugh. He sounded just the way I must have sounded to Randy.

"Listen," I told him. "People steal from business owners with that attitude. As a CEO, you *better* know those numbers. Otherwise, how are you going to know if your CFO's even doing a good job, when you do eventually hire one?"

If you want to get somewhere significant, you have to become familiar with your basic financial documents. They're actually pretty simple. The sheer volume of numbers, the columns and rows, can be intimidating, but once you get past that, there is absolutely nothing difficult or complicated about it. It's basic math, nothing but adding and subtracting.

I thought exactly the same way this guy was thinking, and I'll be forever grateful to Randy for forcing me out of it.

Stay Flexible

My first major mission in Afghanistan, we were supposed to be out in the field for just eighteen hours—but that isn't what happened. We were out there for more than a week. Which was why I didn't have my sniper rifle or range finder with me in the scene I described in chapter 1. And this was not an exception. This was the rule. In the Spec Ops world, missions change constantly.

The same thing happens in business.

If the first principle is all about maintaining an unwavering focus in one direction, this second principle is all about the complementary behavior. Staying focused doesn't mean that focus won't or shouldn't change. It *has* to change. This is the real world, not some theoretical construct in business school class. Circumstances are changing all the time, constantly.

Think of your focus as a building of steel, not concrete: flexible enough to bend with the wind without crumbling.

This is why we train our sniper students not only on moving

targets but also on *unpredictably* moving targets. Sometimes the situation you're observing changes, and you have to make a judgment to shift to a different target. You can't always radio in to command to get new orders when things suddenly change. That's a central part of Special Operations training: we're groomed to be able to make those judgment calls in the field, on the spot, in the moment.

This can happen, and will happen, in your business. You think you're selling *X*, and suddenly you learn that your market wants *Y* and has no use for *X*. Or, you think you've nailed the right demographic for your *X* and suddenly find out that it appeals to a whole different demo. Or that your business model is fundamentally flawed, or has become obsolete.

Make Sure You're in Love with What You Do

This may sound like a strange business directive, but it's essential. In chapter 1, I mentioned that total focus is something that comes from having a near-obsessive passion and dedication for what you're doing. It *has* to. When you decide what you're going to focus on, you better damn well make sure it's something you love, because if it isn't, there's no way you're going to master it. You'll get bored. You'll be distracted, easily knocked off your game. And when you face the big challenges, the really brutal ones, the ones that threaten to knock in your teeth and kick your feet out from under you, you'll just back off and fold your tent.

To run a business effectively, you have to stay on top of an enormous amount of information and material about myriad different aspects of your business. You have to become an expert on your business. How do you do that? There's only one way. It has to be something you really, genuinely enjoy doing. I love writing, I love marketing, I love being engaged in the conceptualization, development, production, and promotion of media. Because I have a passion for every aspect of this business, it doesn't feel onerous or laborious to me. It's work . . . but I love it!

On the other hand, it's *hard* work. If I didn't genuinely enjoy it, to be frank, it would suck. And this is a mistake I see a lot of businesspeople make: working hard at something they don't wholeheartedly enjoy.

In school, my buddy John, the armored vehicle entrepreneur, was never more than a mediocre student. He had no love for academics, and it showed. But once he was in business for himself, he became a voracious student of anything and everything that related to his work. His father, Michael, remembers him sitting on the couch one Christmas morning with several three-inch-thick binders of federal regulations spread out around him, soaking up the information while his daughters played with their presents.

A few years ago, we hired an agency to begin some aggressive paid-acquisition advertising on Facebook. It came really well recommended, and it was clear that the people there knew what they were doing. I could have just written a check. I didn't need to know how the sausages were being made, right? I mean, that's why we hired *them*.

No. I went down to their office and spent half a day with them while they trained me on Facebook in exactly what they do and how. Not so I could do it, but so I could understand it and manage our end of it better. I did that because it fascinates me. It's not simply that I *have* to know it; I *want* to know it.

A year later, I hired a guy who is a whiz at this stuff to come work for us and took the whole process in-house. Now, instead of paying an outside agency to do it, we pay ourselves to do our social media campaigning. We could not have done that if I hadn't taken the time to educate myself so that I understood the process in detail. You can't manage what you don't understand.

Remember that person I mentioned in chapter 1, the woman with the graphic design business? I know why her focus is constantly being distracted by other business opportunities. She doesn't genuinely enjoy the work of running her shop. It's like a burden for her. An albatross around her neck. How is that ever going to work?

I love what I do. Because of that, it's no problem for me to read a dozen or two books a month that could help me expand this business. You might have heard the expression "If you love what you do, it doesn't feel like work." Let's be honest: that isn't true. Work is work, and it takes effort, and sometimes it's excruciatingly hard. So, yeah, it still *feels* like work. But it never feels like *drudge*. It feels exhilarating. It's work, and you feel great doing it. Because of that, you naturally want to dive deep and learn everything about it that you possibly can.

Which is good—because that's the only way you'll survive and thrive.

PROFILE: BETSY MORGAN (THE *HUFFINGTON POST,* THEBLAZE)

In the business world, total situational awareness is about agility and the capacity to adapt to disruption. I don't know anyone who's had more experience thriving in the arena of disruption than Betsy Morgan.

If you had met Betsy when she was twelve and asked her, "What do you want to do when you grow up?" she would have said, "President of the United States." Not from any interest in politics, but from wanting to be in a position where she could have real influence in the world. That hunger has driven her career.

Meet her in person, and you don't feel as if you were talking to a firebrand or radical revolutionary. Thoughtful, intelligent, articulate . . . she might even give you the impression she's the daughter of a New England banker. Which is exactly true. Majored in economics and government at Colby College. Earned her MBA at Harvard Business School. Worked at the Federal Reserve Bank in Boston and tried her hand at investment banking for a stint. Hated it.

"I was a horrible banker," she says. "Just terrible." Knowing Betsy, I doubt that very much. (I don't think she could be *terrible* at anything.) Still, Betsy instinctively understood the first rule of entrepreneurship: if you don't love what you do, you'll never master it.

"If you're going to work eight, ten, twelve hours a day at something, and do it for the rest of your life," she says, "it better be an environment you're excited about, an ecosystem you find fascinating."

For her, that wasn't economics. It was media—and especially television.

Betsy's professional life has been marked by a series of unconventional choices, pivot points she calls "high-risk, high-reward moments." One of those was her decision to stake her claim in the media industry. Betsy had absolutely no background or training in media. She didn't know anyone who worked in it. She grew up watching the same amount of TV as every other kid of the 1980s. There was no logic to her choice. But she loved it. She was fascinated with it. It was that want-to-be-president thing: television was coming into every American home every night, reflecting whatever was going on in the country. Working in television, Betsy felt she could have a very real impact.

In 1997, she landed a job at CBS, working for the office of the chairman, where she got to see all the company's different divisions, from sports to news to its affiliate station business. After a corporate shake-up two years later, she took an executive position at the news division, which was where she was two years after that, when 9/11 happened.

When the first plane hit the North Tower, Betsy could see the smoke from downtown out of her office window. All their reporters rushed downtown, and she lost track of them for hours. A number of the company's engineers who were operating television towers on top of those buildings were killed. It was all very personal.

For the news world, 9/11 was a major and permanent disruption. Suddenly people wanted their news in a constantly available stream. For the next ten days straight, the network stayed on the air, commercial-free, 24/7. Betsy had two couches in her office; she would catch some sleep on one, and the head of CBSNews.com (who reported to Betsy) slept on the other couch. Everyone lived at the office until they could put their heads up and the country gradually started going back to normal.

Except there wasn't really any "normal" to go back to. Getting news a few times a night was over. Twenty-four/seven was here to stay. To the broadcast news networks, CNN seemed like an eight-hundred-pound gorilla that threatened their existing model with its round-the-clock coverage. But of course, the real eight-hundred-pound gorilla wasn't cable.

It was the Internet.

In the years following 9/11, Betsy saw a new breed of media giant emerging: the AOLs, Yahoos, Googles. She started going out to Silicon Valley regularly, getting to know the players. She attended Google's earliest Zeitgeist conferences. She networked. She did something most of her colleagues weren't doing: she paid attention to what was happening—and to what was coming over the horizon.

Betsy was an anomaly in the television world. She was not trained as a producer, had not been a communications major in college. She was essentially schooled through on-the-job training and her own raging curiosity. (I relate.) She was also by this time a senior executive, and one of the beauties of her unique position there at CBS News was that she could roam where she wanted and more or less make her own schedule. She had free rein to follow her curiosity and appetite for learning.

One day she took two young Google engineers she'd befriended around the offices of the CBS Broadcast Center in Hell's Kitchen. These guys had developed a cool digital tool they called Google Trends, which revealed how often and when and where people searched for a given term. Betsy thought it was incredible. She had these guys demo the product for top producers at every one of CBS's news shows and raved about its potential.

"This is fantastic!" she told them. "With real-time data, you could change your lineups for that evening's six-thirty news broadcast, based on what's trending on Google that day. Just imagine what the investigative reporters at *60 Minutes* or *48 Hours* could do with this! You'll see connections to things that you never would have seen before, as a normal course of investigating or sourcing a story!"

Every single one of the producers was skeptical. "I can't believe you wasted our time with this crap," said one. They didn't need to know what people were searching. Their careers were built on setting the news agenda, not having the audience do it.

Betsy knew it was time to leave CBS. But go where? She didn't want to join another big established media company. She wanted to go where the disruption was happening.

Before long, she was approached by people from an upstart blog-based news aggregator who were looking for a CEO. Practically the opposite of the venerable CBS News, this venture was barely a year old and had fairly little traffic. At CBS, Betsy had hundreds of people reporting to her; this new company's total staff numbered thirty. It was called the *Huffington Post*.

Betsy took the job.

In her last meeting with CBS's CEO, Les Moonves, he said, "Betsy, I'm sad you're leaving, but I understand, you've been here a long time. But, the *Huffington Post*? I really think you've made the wrong choice here, and I hope you'll reconsider. Is anyone in the news business going to take this startup seriously?"

"Leslie, I appreciate that," Betsy replied, "but the decision's made. They're about to announce my new job in the *New York Times*." Twenty minutes later, the *Times* edition with that story hit the streets.

Under Betsy's leadership, the *Huffington Post* grew rapidly, in both audience and revenue, and she and the three founders got to participate in the creation of a new model. Part of the newness of it was the three-stranded braid of its content: roughly equal parts opinion pieces, reporting, and content curation—that is, the collecting and distillation (aggregation) of news from other sources.

But it was more than that. What Betsy was seeing at the *Huffington Post* wasn't an *audience* so much as a *community*. The first concept is passive; the second is active. This was what her bosses at CBS News couldn't fathom: a news organization in which the audience's point of view was a driving force. When Walter Cronkite closed each day's newscast throughout the 1960s and 1970s by saying, "And that's the way it is," for millions of Americans, that's the way it *was*. Not anymore. Now viewers wanted to have a say in "the way it is."

As exciting as her tenure at Arianna Huffington's new and very successful company was, Betsy wasn't finished surprising the people who knew her. Barely two years later, she left *HuffPost* to look for the next disruption. Her next move stunned everyone. In late 2010, the news broke that she was taking a job as president of a brand-new multimedia news and opinion startup called TheBlaze, created by the controversial and recently departed Fox News commentator Glenn Beck.

If Betsy's friends were baffled when she left her cherry post at CBS News to join an uncertain upstart, now their heads practically exploded. To many observers, the move from Arianna Huffington's left-leaning media organization to join forces with Glenn Beck gave them whiplash.

To Betsy, it made perfect sense. It was a chance to pioneer more disruption.

People were looking for media brands they could feel a personal affinity with, brands that seemed to align with their own values. The *Huffington Post* was one of the first major news organizations to say unapologetically, "This is what we believe." The audience craved that kind of voice, and mainstream media weren't delivering it. Glenn was doing the same thing.

I haven't asked him, but I imagine it must have seemed like a hell of a stretch from Glenn's point of view, too. Here's this Harvard grad who had worked for the Federal Reserve, CBS News, and Arianna freaking Huffington! Talk about the perfect recipe for a conservative's nightmare. Betsy says he "had to be pulled kicking and screaming" to their first meeting. But within minutes of meeting each other, the two had a connection.

"Arianna never talked politics with me," says Betsy, "and Glenn never talked politics with me." It wasn't about politics. It was about a new way of doing media.

Just as when she went to *Huffington,* Betsy had tons of people tell her that Beck's thing would never work. His audience was too old; it wasn't tech savvy enough to create a strong digital viewership. Beck was too radical, too opinionated. People would never pay a monthly fee to get that content. And on and on.

It was like CBS News all over again.

"Which, to be honest, I sort of thrive on," says Betsy. "Tell me it can't be done, and I can't wait to prove otherwise!"

All those naysayers weren't stupid. They didn't lack intellectual sophistication. But they were wrong. What they lacked was *situational awareness*. They hadn't paid close attention to what was going on. Betsy had.

Betsy stayed at TheBlaze for four and a half years, during which time she grew the site to a Quantcast top fifty Web site as she built its television stream's paid-subscription model, which has since become the de facto industry standard for paid-subscription operations.

I've learned a ton from Betsy. A few years ago, I persuaded her to join our advisory board at Hurricane, and we're lucky to have her. Today she is one of the most highly regarded thought leaders in digital media. She's still watching it all, still paying attention to what's over the horizon. I can't wait to see what she does next.

Chapter 3
VIOLENCE OF ACTION

✦ ✦ ✦

magine you are on a plane flying at, say, twelve thousand feet. The flight is smooth; the view is great. You get out of your seat, step over to chat with a colleague. Just another ordinary day. Then you step over to the open hatch.

And throw yourself out of the plane.

I'll never forget the first time I did this. As a new SEAL, I had lost a good friend, Mike Bearden, in a parachute training accident. Now it was my turn to be trained to skydive, and I'd be lying if I said there wasn't a little voice in the back of my mind trying to talk me out of it. Another guy in my jump class let that same little voice get to him. "That's it," he said after taking one look out that open hatch. "I'm out." He sat down again, and that was that. He wasn't budging from his seat until we got back on terra firma.

I understood where he was coming from. It's a sobering thing, looking out at the world from cloud level. We have an expression in jump school, "Why would you want to throw yourself out of a perfectly good airplane?" and it's only partially a joke. There is nothing quite like the experience of jumping out of an airplane at twelve thousand feet. It's not something you can ease yourself into or try out for a bit to see what it feels like before you decide to commit all the way. You can't float a trial period, run a straw poll, or hire a focus group. You can't test out a beta version.

All you can do is jump.

So I did.

The next moment I was in the air, with twelve thousand feet of empty space below me.

Years later, I thought back on that moment. It was the middle of 2006, and I was about to throw myself out the hatch of another plane, only not the kind that flies through the sky. After thirteen-plus years of life in the service, I was about to leave the military.

The past few months I'd been taking stock of things. As course master of the SEAL sniper program, I'd had a great career. But my fun meter was pegged, my knees were a wreck, and my back hurt constantly. (The life of a SEAL is not exactly easy on the body.) I did some simple retirement math: if I stuck around another seven years, which would put me at the requisite twenty years in (what it takes to receive a pension based on 50 percent of your base pay), or another twelve, putting me at an even twenty-five (which gets you 75 percent of base pay), I would be not only physically broken but financially broke as well. As a Navy SEAL, I had great income because of all the "special pays" added onto my base pay, but only my base pay would factor into what I got paid on retirement. In essence, I would get the same retirement as a navy cook. (No offense, cooks.)

There were guys who thought I was crazy to even think about

leaving before I'd qualified for full retirement, even some who were angry at me for it. But I wanted a better life for my family, and for myself, too.

Still, it felt a lot like that moment when I gazed out the plane's open hatch at twelve thousand feet. I was about to leave a known environment and structure with its fixed routine and black-and-white rules. I had lived my entire adult life in the military. Tomorrow morning I would wake up to find myself in a totally different world, a world where the only real rule was that there were no rules. I could understand and exploit that sort of environment as an unconventional warfare operator working in overseas theaters—but back home, in civilian life? Totally new territory to me. *This must be what it's like when you get out of prison,* I thought. I was scared shitless.

Okay, Webb, I told myself. *It's a simple three-step process.*

One: *Open the hatch.*

Two: *Look out at twelve thousand feet of air.*

Three: *Jump.*

I jumped. It was one of the best decisions I ever made.

SEALs are famous for their intense physical training, but what most don't fully grasp is that surviving BUD/S and the rest of SEAL training is less about your physical ability and more about your mind-set and habits of operation. To a SEAL, there is no such thing as doing something halfway, or even nine-tenths of the way. There is only full-on doing. Storming the castle.

Violence of action is where front sight focus and total situational awareness come together in a moment of decisive initiative, swift as a bullet and just as deadly. Do your homework, take every factor into account you possibly can, focus unwaveringly on your target—and once the instant for action appears, act boldly and without hesitation.

General George Patton put it this way: "A good plan violently executed *now* is better than a perfect plan executed next week."

There's a reason they call a business leader the chief "executive." Smart planning is important, but the crucial point is that you have to *execute* the plan, period. Wait too long in combat, and you'll find yourself dead. Do this in business, and you'll find yourself out of business.

To give you a sense of what I mean by violence of action in the context of business, let me walk you through some initiatives we began at Hurricane Group in our first few years.

Violence of action is burned into the DNA of Hurricane, right down to the name.

Although I did not adopt the Hurricane Group umbrella structure until the spring of 2013, that impulse we call "business by storm" was driving our operation right from its earliest days. My fledgling team and I launched SOFREP in February 2012. Within thirty days, we'd launched a second site.

Back in 2011, when I was working part-time for that other military site, I had a few guys who wrote for me. One of them, a former Army Ranger turned novelist and journalist, came with me to SOFREP. Jack Murphy was a talented writer and proved to be a golden asset to SOFREP; today he serves as our editor in chief as well as a roving reporter in trouble spots around the world. (More on that in chapter 4.)

The month before launching SOFREP, Jack and I went to the

annual SHOT (Shooting Hunting Outdoor Trade) Show in Las Vegas and were surprised to find ourselves greeted almost like celebrities. We realized we had a significant following of gearheads from the blog we'd been doing, and we couldn't serve them adequately in the pages of SOFREP. So in March we launched the Loadout Room (LoadoutRoom.com), a review site covering gear and the adventure lifestyle—"extreme reviews for the everyday adventurer," our tagline goes. As of this writing, the site gets a few hundred thousand unique visitors per month. Not SOFREP-level traffic, but not bad.

It wasn't long before we launched a third site, the Arms Guide (TheArmsGuide.com), as "the place to learn about all things firearms in a friendly and professional setting." After the site had been up for a while, we started getting major pressure from mainstream advertisers who were nervous because of all the Second Amendment and gun violence controversy, so we let it lie fallow and stopped updating its content. Still, it kept getting a ton of traffic. Eventually, we reactivated it and brought on a dedicated writer for the site. Within two months, we took it from thirty thousand uniques to over a hundred thousand.

We launched a fourth. I noticed there was no Web site dealing authentically with military and law enforcement aviation. There were all kinds of fanboy-type aviation sites, but no serious aviation-focused site with a Spec Ops point of view. Aviation is one of my passions and the topic felt personal, so we started FighterSweep .com. We brought on board some really good writers who were also pilots and started seeing solid engagement in the site right away, especially from the active-duty community. One day the wing commander of some air force squadron commented on one of our articles, and it kind of blew my mind.

There were other sites, too, more than a dozen in all, some of which we stood up and then retired again when they didn't take off. But it wasn't just Web sites. In our first year, we also began launching other types of media initiatives, starting with SOFREP Radio.

Early in 2012, I was a guest on someone's podcast, and when he saw the kind of audience we drew, he encouraged me to start a podcast of our own. So we did. In mid-June, we published our first SOFREP Radio podcast. It immediately shot to No. 1 in its category (government) on iTunes and stayed there. We've kept it going weekly, and it's been in the No. 1 spot or somewhere in the top ten ever since. We've had a huge range of guests—Spec Ops vets, bestselling authors, prizewinning journalists, characters from Chris Kyle to Buzz Aldrin. As of this writing, we've got nearly 250 episodes online.

Then there was SOFREP TV. We started out that first spring with a video series, *Inside the Team Room*, that featured a group of Spec Ops vets gathered around a pitcher of beer, talking about their experiences. It was enormously popular and sparked a series of sequels and spin-offs. We did a *Team Room* series with SEALs, one with Green Berets, one with Army Rangers. We flew to Poland to shoot a piece with GROM, the Polish Spec Ops unit. We talked to members of the British and Rhodesian SAS (Special Air Service).

Then we decided to raise the bar on ourselves and relaunch our video offering as a paid service, the Spec Ops Channel. My goal with this one is to disrupt the whole cable-military-history-content space. In other words, to scare the crap out of Discovery Channel, Nat Geo Channel, and A&E's History channel. As of this writing, we're gearing up to launch in early 2017. We'll see what happens.

And of course, no media company would be complete without a publishing branch.

In September 2012, we published *No Easy Op*, the first in a "World Report" series that covered breaking news as it related to military, intelligence, and foreign affairs. *No Easy Op* was a short e-book discussing the content and circumstances of a newly released firsthand account of the operation that killed bin Laden, itself titled *No Easy Day*. On the heels of *No Easy Op* came *Ranger Knowledge* (August 2013), *Africa Lost* (August 2013), *The Syria Report* (November 2013), *Operation Red Wings* (December 2013), *Navy SEALs BUD/S Preparation Guide* (April 2014), and *The ISIS Solution* (November 2014).

But the book that put SOFREP publishing on the map was our May 2014 release, *Benghazi: The Definitive Report*, which hit the *New York Times* bestseller list.

Most of the titles listed above we published with St. Martin's Press (SMP). Ever since SMP bought my first book, *The Red Circle*, I'd had a close relationship with our editor there, Marc Resnick. At the same time, I was bringing a lot of military authors to Marc for their own book deals, including Mike Ritland (*Trident K9 Warriors*) and Nick Irving (*The Reaper*), who both became breakout sensations and huge bestsellers. After *Benghazi* (which we published as a one-off through William Morrow), we started talking with Marc about establishing our own imprint with SMP so we could really help our guys and have a solid outlet for these stories that needed telling. In 2016, we published our first book together under the SMP/SOFREP Books imprint, *Raising Men*, by my BUD/S teammate and sniper school training partner, Eric Davis, and had close to another dozen books in the pipeline.

But I wasn't happy. It wasn't enough. I felt we were still bottlenecked.

While I was in Europe for that fact-finding "vacation" in the summer of 2016, I read a handful of books, including Richard Branson's *Losing My Virginity*, in which he talks about Virgin Records and the various distribution deals he put together. I put that book down and thought, *We need to be our own label.*

So that's what we'll do next. It'll probably be the end of 2017 before I can hire the team to put behind it, but we're going to become our own publisher. We'll start with a hundred titles. And then see where it goes.

One more initiative: the clubs.

In November 2015, we had a company strategy meeting and pulled in the members of our advisory board to brief them on our plans and ask for ideas. One of our advisers asked, "Why aren't you doing a gear club?" We had a huge existing audience coming to us and asking for information and advice on what to buy. We saw how well Birchbox and a handful of other box-subscription businesses were doing. Instead of just giving our readers advice and having them go buy from other vendors, why not do our own subscription box?

We knew absolutely nothing about this business model. That, of course, only made it more interesting. (It's called "violence of action," not "violence of contemplation.") We launched the SOFREP Crate Club in January. By June, we were on a run rate to do well over $3 million in revenue, just on the box business.

So I said, "Let's do books, too."

People were coming to us asking for good titles to read. So we launched the SOFREP Book Club. This is not your typical discount-type book-of-the-month club. We pick books that we like, in some cases first run, hot off the press, and we also create a community around the books themselves and, periodically, a live experience.

We did our first live event in the spring of 2016, when we had

Dick Marcinko, the legendary bad-boy founder of SEAL Team Six and author of the bestselling *Rogue Warrior* series, come speak to a packed house of SOFREP Book Club members. It was a great way to inaugurate the series. You can see highlights of Marcinko's visit with us on the Spec Ops Channel.

So there you go. What started in February 2012 as a blog within a few years became a network of Web sites, a podcast, a video channel, a monthly gear subscription company, a book club community, and a publishing house. That's how Hurricane Group happened: one part plan, ten parts execution.

Violence of action.

Get off the *X*

In the SEAL teams, violence of action typically means using the element of surprise to overwhelm the enemy to the point of immediate submission. Assaulting a compound in the Afghanistan hills, we would pour into that place like a tidal wave—kick open a door, toss in a flashbang (stun grenade), and have everyone in the room zip-tied and blinded by a hood over the head before a single one of them was awake enough to complete a thought.

The term "violence" in this context doesn't mean busting people up or tearing around, breaking things. (No actual physical violence was used in scenarios like the one I just described, unless some foolhardy soul put up resistance, in which case he would simply get a muzzle *pop!* in the chest to quiet him down.) Violence refers to the speed of action.

Actually, to be more accurate, it's not speed but *velocity*. Speed is simply doing something fast, but not necessarily doing the right things fast. You can be in a rush and screw everything up. (Speedy but ineffective.) Velocity is speed plus direction. In other words, not just fast action, but *directed* fast action. That kind of rapid, focused action is what would give us the edge in any assault operation.

It's also one of our trade secrets at Hurricane. When we do something, we do it fast, typically faster than anyone expects, because we don't accept industry norms. (Remember: norm = average = mediocre.) Not long ago, we had to put up a new landing page for a fairly sophisticated marketing initiative. The woman who was editing copy for us expected that we'd need a week or ten days to get it completed, coded, and live online. We had it up in two days. "I've worked for a lot of companies," she told me, "including some major brand names. I've never seen anyone do something like that even half as fast as you guys did."

"I know," I said. "That's why I've been pushing so hard for content." For us, that's normal.

I was talking recently with Hoby Darling, CEO of Skullcandy, who prior to Skull was an executive at Nike, and Hoby said something interesting about velocity. Years earlier, when he had worked for a small athletic-wear startup, he saw that everyone in the company was afraid of Nike, this big monster company with all these resources that they didn't have.

"Later, when I found myself running a division of Nike," he said, "I realized we'd had it upside down. Now I was working for the big monster, and what we were all afraid of was the small startups, because we knew they could outmaneuver us and execute much faster."

We have an expression in the SEALs, "Get off the X." The moment you take fire, you want to get away from the point of contact. You don't want the enemy targeting you; you want to maneuver around to where you are targeting the enemy.

Here's how I see it, though: In business, the "enemy" is not the other companies in your field. Here, the real enemy is mediocrity and complacency. Blockbuster wasn't destroyed by Netflix; it was destroyed by its own inertia and irrelevance. The digital revolution happened, and it failed to get off the X quickly enough to survive the hit.

Take the Shot

As important as it is to act quickly, here is what is even more important: to act, period.

During the stalking (stealth and concealment) phase of the Navy SEAL sniper course, students are trained to sneak up unobserved to within meters of their instructors, experienced snipers who are looking for them with high-powered optics, and take a shot, either a blank or, in some cases, a live round fired at a steel target. When I was the head instructor of the program, it amazed me how often I saw students make the stalk successfully, get within range, set up position for firing on their target with time to spare, *but never take the shot*. They would be sitting there in their FFP (final firing position), checking and rechecking their camouflage, going back over their mental checklist to make sure they hadn't overlooked anything and were as sure as they could be that they would not be detected when they actually took their shot. And they would still be doing that when their time allotment ran out.

There is no "close" or "almost" here, only pass or fail. In the course, "fail" meant they were sent home, never to become snipers. On the battlefield, "fail" means someone dies.

In business, here in the civilian world, I see the same thing happen all the time. I see people trapped in bad jobs they hate, careers they're unhappy with. They know what to do but fail to take action.

I have a friend I'll call Dan, a software engineer, about fifty years old. Dan is always on the verge of doing this big thing. "I'm going to sell my rental property," he says, "and get out and make a change." He's been saying this for three years. It hasn't happened—and it never will, not unless and until he pulls the trigger. He's a victim of his own paralysis by analysis.

Dan has been interviewing for a better job for a while, but so far nothing's worked out.

I tell him, "Dan, you're fifty years old. No one's going to hire you. They're going to hire someone younger for less. Why don't you just buy a business and get out of this rut you're in?"

He tells me he's got some sort of tax thing going on with the IRS and he's just waiting for it to get straightened out.

I say, "That's just a bullshit excuse, man. Everything you're saying is nothing but a smoke screen for the fact that you're not taking action. You've got to pull the trigger."

Dan is like a lot of people I see: making reasonably decent money—$150,000, maybe $200,000 a year—but in debt up to their asses and just getting painted farther into a corner. They know what they have to do. They just don't do it.

I see this in entrepreneurs, too, like the graphic design shop owner I mentioned earlier. She has a business partner whom she leans on a lot, because she doesn't really love the business herself. She wants out but feels stuck.

"Look," I say, "it's not a problem that this thing hasn't worked out. I test things all the time that turn out not to work. I've stood up Web sites that have been complete flops. But you have to be able to say, 'Okay, that didn't work,' and take *action*."

Honestly, the best thing for her would be to just get out, right now. Walk away. But she won't do it.

One of our Web developers who lives in the Philippines tells me how they trap monkeys in his country. They dig a hole and place a coconut in there. The monkey reaches into the hole and grabs the coconut, and once he's grabbed it, his fist is too big to pull back out. He's trapped.

All he has to do is let go of the coconut. But he won't unclench his fist.

Remind you of anyone you know?

Make Action Your Default Mode

There's a phrase from psychology that people sometimes use in business: "a bias for action." That describes perfectly the SEAL mentality. Given the choice to do something or sit there, we'll always favor taking action.

Just to be clear: a bias for action doesn't mean that you *always* pull the trigger, in every situation and circumstance. That's just being headstrong. There are times when the smart thing to do is to wait and watch. (Again: observation and reconnaissance.) Sometimes a situation needs a certain amount of time to ripen before you can see clearly what the right next move is. So no, having a bias for action doesn't mean you shoot off your mouth at every turn and jump off every cliff you see, and it doesn't mean making impulsive decisions.

It simply means that taking action is your default mode. That when you're given a range of options, your first choice is to act rather than sit back. Which puts you in the minority, because most people have a bias for *inaction*. (Inertia = mediocrity = the Law of Most.) By having a bias for action, you have an automatic edge over everyone else in the field.

Although I've had a rocky relationship with my dad, he has also inspired me in many ways. His dogged self-taught entrepreneurialism is one; his bias for action is another. He and my mom talked for years about taking the family on a boat and sailing around the world. So what; lots of people talk. Only he didn't just talk. He said, "I don't want to be the guy who keeps talking about taking this sailing trip but never actually takes it. I'm going to untie the boat and sail away on the journey." And son of a bitch, he did. Suddenly we were all out on the Pacific, heading for Tahiti.

This is what I learned from my father: untie the boat and go.

A bias for action means that your preferred way of learning is to learn through doing, rather than to try to get the learning done *before* you start the doing. In every one of the initiatives I described above, from our weekly podcast to our monthly Crate Club to our paid TV channel, we've started out not really knowing anything about how to do it. Not because we're brash and impulsive, or that we act without forethought or any preparation at all, but because we have a very high preset of expectations.

My time in the SEAL teams expanded my view of what is possible. In the teams, you quickly realize that most people have preset limits on what they believe is normal and possible and that most are capable of at least three to four times the output they think they are.

My guess is, by virtue of the fact that you picked this book up and have read this far, that includes you.

Create Action-Focused Work Habits

For my twenty-sixth birthday on June 26, 2000, I got something that is to this day one of my most prized possessions: a certificate stating I'd successfully completed the Naval Special Warfare (SEAL) scout sniper program. The signature on that certificate reads "Captain William H. McRaven." Captain McRaven was on hand to officiate.

Fourteen years later, McRaven, now a four-star admiral, delivered the commencement address at the University of Texas, in a widely circulated speech called "If You Want to Change the World." In it he talks about ten lessons he learned in the course of SEAL training that he offers up as behaviors that can change the world. The first is this: *Every morning, make your bed.*

This is the man who organized and executed Operation Neptune Spear, the Spec Ops mission that killed Osama bin Laden. A month after giving that address, he was appointed commander of SOCOM, the entire U.S. Special Operations Command. When this guy talks about changing the world, he's not just making noise. (The whole speech is worth watching. Just google "McRaven make your bed.")

His point? If I look through your bedroom and poke around your kitchen, I don't need to see your financials, because I already have a pretty good idea of what kind of shape your business is in. The

Buddhists have an expression: "How you do anything is how you do everything." How you manage the smallest mundane details of your life will add up to your success—or failure—on the largest scale.

Winston Churchill ran the war effort in an underground complex called the Cabinet War Rooms in London. You can still visit the war room today, and when you do, you'll see his desk, preserved in his office. On it sits a box with a label that says, "Action This Day." Notice, Churchill didn't have an IN-box. He had a TODAY box. He also didn't clock out at five in the afternoon. Didn't matter if it was midnight, or two in the morning, the man didn't leave his desk until he'd handled the last thing in that box.

Develop the habit of doing it now. Refuse to let yourself procrastinate.

Never Use Money (or Lack of Money) as an Excuse

I hear people talk about this great idea they have that would be a huge success, if they just had the funding to get it off the ground. Worst bullshit excuse ever. What makes this hackneyed rationale so destructive is not that they say it but that they believe it.

Money, or lack of money, is never the problem. It's what people use as an excuse to avoid facing the real problem, which is unwillingness to take action.

The most surprising thing to me about financing in business has been how insanely available it is. The Small Business Administration (SBA), for example, presents a low-risk way to borrow money from the government to buy or start a business.

A few years ago, I needed some working capital to invest in a few key personnel I wanted to hire to help take us to the next level. I went to a billionaire friend in the city and explained what I wanted to do.

He listened to my pitch, nodded his head, and said, "Okay, that all sounds good. So go borrow the money."

"What do you mean, borrow the money?" I said. "I was going to *raise* it!" (From him, of course, though I hadn't gotten to that part yet.)

He looked at me and said, "Brandon. Why raise the money when you can just borrow it?"

Shit, I thought. *That's a really good point.*

I went to the SBA, got a loan application, forced myself to sit down and go through all the rigmarole of filling it out, and submitted it. Ninety days later, I had $250,000.

Yes, I hate filling out forms as much as you do. Get over it.

Not that working capital is always to be had at the snap of your fingers and filling out of a form. Sometimes getting the funding you need takes a little creativity.

I recently went to a bank looking for a line of credit to do a specific advertising campaign. This is a bank that lends to companies with box-subscription programs like our Crate Club.

"Wow," the guy said after he'd finished looking our business over. "You own the business, you make a profit, and you've got great growth. However, we typically lend to companies that lose money but are venture backed."

I said, "Why would you do that? They *lose money.*"

"Well, yeah," he said, "they lose money, but they have venture capital behind them, so if things go wrong, we hope that the VC will save them."

I have to admit I could not compute what the hell he was saying.

"But . . . we're *profitable*," I said. "We're hitting all our numbers. We just want access to a little capital to grow this same program further. We know what we're doing, we know it's fully scalable, and we know how to turn the dial and make more money with it."

"Yeah, I know, that makes perfect sense," he said. "It's just against our lending parameters."

I said, "So wait. You're saying you guys only loan money to companies that are growing but losing money, on a wing and a prayer that their VC backers will keep pumping money in if the shit hits the fan and it all goes south?"

He nodded and smiled. "Yeah. Pretty much."

At this point, I felt as if I were in a freaking Ayn Rand novel. Some bureaucratic banking officer was telling me he couldn't loan us money because our model worked and our business was thriving? (And we wonder how Wall Street crashed?)

The hell with it, I said. *We'll do it ourselves.*

I gathered up all my credit cards and built a credit card system: we spend up to the limit, then pay it off and hit the next one. Using all my personal credit, plus one company business card, we essentially arbitraged ourselves up to spending a good half a million dollars on Facebook. Worked just fine.

Don't get me wrong; I'm not saying that this would have been a smart thing for us to do in year one. It wouldn't have. It makes sense now only because we've been in business for a while and we know from past performance that what we have going works and we've proven its scalability.

Be Confident—Not Arrogant

People often think of Spec Ops guys as people with a ton of attitude. You know: swagger, overconfidence. But that's the movies, not the reality. In the real world of combat, swagger gets you killed, and probably a bunch of your buddies with you. In business, you may not get physically blown up, but you will get fiscally blown up.

SEALs do have a level of confidence that is unusual and unshakable. But that's not attitude—the opposite, in fact. You have to be open-minded, to be able to listen. Be flexible. Adapt. I have very strong opinions, but I can also pivot on a dime and completely change my viewpoint, even a long-held opinion, if someone presents a clear and cogent argument for it.

When Chris Kyle published his memoir, *American Sniper,* he wrote about an encounter with Jesse Ventura that Ventura claimed never happened. The dispute ended up in court. Then Chris was killed, but if you thought that would end the lawsuit, you were wrong, because Ventura continued to press the suit against Chris's widow, Taya.

The SEAL community was outraged. This guy is going to sue Chris Kyle's widow?! It seemed as total a betrayal of the brotherhood as you could think of. For weeks, we had people venting on the pages of SOFREP and on our SOFREP Radio interviews. And then I did something I don't think anyone on the planet expected.

I had Jesse on the podcast as my guest. Not only that, but I didn't attack him.

To be fair (to me, I mean), I did hold his feet to the fire. But I was respectful throughout. Some of our readers were incensed with me, which I completely understand. Chris was a friend. Did I think suing his widow was the right thing to do? Are you kidding me? I thought it was as low as it gets. But here's the thing: the man still deserved to be heard.

Having a strong opinion is one thing. I have plenty of those. (Ask anyone who knows me.) But having a point of view doesn't mean you close your mind. If you don't maintain a genuinely open and curious mind, if you don't listen carefully to the cues and clues around you, to the input of your team and the advice of your best advisers, then your violence of action stands a good chance of being impulsive and/or misguided, which will kill you dead, and sooner than you expect. The only way you can employ violence of action effectively is by coupling it with a thoughtful, open mind and a reliable ability to put your ego in the backseat.

This isn't easy. I'm not going to pretend I don't have a big ego, and I'm also not going to pretend *you* don't have one. That's normal; in fact, it's essential. Who ever heard of a successful entrepreneur without a healthy ego? It's your passion, your drive, your ambition, and your aspirations that make this thing work. That's all your ego.

But you can't let your ego drive the car. You have to be able to put it, if not in the backseat, at least over in the passenger seat.

Then who drives the car? Your better judgment, fueled by total situational awareness—that is, by doing your homework.

Plan for Disaster So It Won't Be a Disaster When It Happens (Because It *Will* Happen)

I don't just jump out of planes; I also fly them. Flying is one of my three favorite pastimes (the others being skiing and surfing). I don't own a car, but I own several planes. If you follow me on social media, you'll see a constant stream of photographs snapped from over the Statue of Liberty, Manhattan skyline, and other New York landmarks.

Here's the main thing you need to know about flying: it's not a casual activity. You can hop in your car and drive off on impulse without thinking much about it. Doesn't work that way with a plane. Climb into the cockpit of even a fairly small, simple plane, and you'll notice it looks a hell of a lot more complicated than the dashboard of your car. That's because it *is* a hell of a lot more complicated. There are a hundred things you have to check before you leave the runway. Preflight routine is no joke. If you don't have backup plans for your backup plans, you can end up dead before the day is out.

Running a business is a lot like flying a plane.

Again—and this is worth repeating—violence of action does *not* mean being careless, acting on impulse, or committing to a course of action without forethought. If anything, it's the opposite. The only way you can genuinely give yourself over to violence of action is if you are as prepared as a human being can possibly be. That's why this chapter is preceded by a chapter called "Total Situational Awareness."

Contingency planning is an essential part of any mission, because inevitably something will go wrong. In the 2011 raid on bin Laden's compound, the team that went in suddenly lost one of their helicopters. That could have been catastrophic—but it wasn't, because the SEALs had a contingency plan in place, which they executed. They didn't waste any time running in circles or freaking out. They blew up the downed chopper, went on with the mission, and got everyone out of there without losing a single member of the team.

Whether you're flying a plane, assaulting an enemy compound, or launching a business initiative, you want to plan for as many contingency outcomes as you can think of so you'll know what to do when it all goes sideways. Because if you have to stop and think about it when it happens, you're screwed.

You find this out really fast when your business is digital and depends on an uninterrupted online presence. Servers crash; hosting issues happen. At SOFREP, we learned really fast that it's worth the money to pay for excellent hosting.

In 2015, Facebook tightened up its guidelines on who can advertise on its site. At the time, we had a landing page—not the Facebook ad itself, but only the landing page that you clicked through to from the ad—that featured a picture of a Gerber multi-tool with its saw blade flipped open. Facebook interpreted that as a weapon and killed our entire ad set. Not just that ad. Our entire ad set.

It was maddening. As far as we could see, we were in full compliance with its guns-and-knives policy. But without warning, we were shut down.

By this time, Facebook advertising had become a central plank in our business model, and at the moment we happened to be having a really good run. Having the whole ad campaign shut down cost us a *lot* of money. It took a few days to get hold of a representative, find out what the problem was, get it fixed, and get that particular ad back into compliance. It hit our cash flow hard.

I know we can't afford to have that happen again. As I write this, in the fall of 2016, we're preparing for the holidays, which we know are going to be big for us this year. We anticipate taking down as much as $50,000 a day in new revenue. We cannot afford to have the whole thing go dark. Going into this season, we knew we needed a contingency plan, so we designed a separate landing page, with its own URL and an alternative ad set attached to a different credit card on our advertising accounts with plenty of credit on it, ready to plug in and go. Now, if anything unforeseen goes wrong and something interrupts our ad campaign again, we can immediately switch on our backup system.

Understand: we're not *running* these ads. The entire alternate system is just sitting there. We'll most likely never use it. It's like having a backup generator in case the power goes out. It took a lot of work to build, but it was worth it, even if all it does is sit there and we never have to use it.

By the way, this is one reason not to be afraid of failure: often failure, crises, and setbacks are the only way you gain that invaluable insight you need to anticipate future problems and design the right contingencies. Which is another reason an imperfect plan executed *now* is so vastly superior to a perfect plan executed sometime in the vague future. Your imperfect plan will lead to some gains and probably some setbacks, too—which will give you exactly the information you need to design a more perfect plan for the next move.

Don't Be Afraid to Pull the Plug

One of the most important decisions you'll ever make is the one when you say, "I'm pulling the plug—*now*."

There is a world of difference between failing and quitting. The concept "quit" simply isn't in my vocabulary. But failing? That's something else entirely. You can't be a winner, in my book, without having drunk deeply from the well of insight and humility that comes with failing. And while I don't condone quitting under any circumstances, there are times when the smartest move is a tactical retreat.

I told you about the winners our company launched—the Load-out Room, the Arms Guide, Fighter Sweep, the Spec Ops Channel—but there were losers, too. I've stood up at least half a dozen new sites at Hurricane that haven't worked out.

We created a site for military spouses called Military Posh. I still believe that space has potential, but at the time we couldn't get it right, or at least not fast enough. My model is, start a site, do our best to build it, and if it doesn't grow or we can't figure out some way to monetize it adequately, then we kill it. Typically, you'll know within six months whether or not a site is working. In the case of Military Posh, the page views just weren't there, and we weren't able to get the sponsors we needed. So after six months, we shelved it. We might find the right sponsor at some point; it's still there, and we could have it back online in no time. But for now, it's mothballed.

We started another site, Transition Hero, a military-to-civilian transition advice and jobs portal for vets, the only one of its kind on the Internet. We had a sponsor for a while, but we lost them and didn't have the manpower to maintain the site properly without any solid ad revenue. I really believe in that concept and have high hopes that we'll find a way to bring it back at some point. But I had to yank it. As with Military Posh, we took a loss on that one, but it wasn't huge, because we hadn't poured a great deal of investment into it.

For a while, we had a site called Hit the Woodline, a satirical blog in the style of the *Onion*, about military life. This was one of the few sites that we bought as an already-existing property and brought under our umbrella. I paid about fifteen grand for it, but we never found the right person to run it, so it, too, is sitting on the inactive shelf.

I spent even more on SpecialOperations.com, which I bought for forty-five grand. To be clear, that $45,000 outlay was just for the domain name. Once we owned it, we scraped the site clean and started over from scratch—analogous to buying a physical property for the land and road frontage, tearing the existing structure down, and rebuilding from the foundation up.

I worked with NavySEALs.com for a while, a site run by my friend and former SEAL Mark Divine. Mark is a great guy and it's a fine site, but once we built the site and Facebook page to over a million followers, he took it independent again. I've tested out bringing other popular blogs into our network and monetizing them, too, but found that a lot of these smaller site owners had unrealistic expectations and lacked business experience, which caused problems. They thought they were going to make money right away, and it just doesn't happen that way. Eventually, I decided it wasn't worth the headache and that we should stick to investing in our own properties.

My point here is that every single one of these sites was a great idea, and I could have easily kept them going for a lot longer than I did—they could still be going today, draining our cash, our effort, and our focus—if I didn't have a strong belief in recognizing when something's not working and calling a tactical retreat. *Fast.*

My six-month yardstick generally works well for our Web sites, in part because the ongoing operational cost is not that high; if you were keeping open a retail storefront, it might be very different. Every project has its own tolerances and critical metrics. You have to establish your own key performance indicators, whether it's revenue targets or traffic goals or profitability (or the break-even point) or whatever matters most, and decide ahead of time how long you'll give it before you pull the plug. And then follow your plan.

You have to get off the X.

PROFILE: AMIT VERMA (THE VERMA GROUP)

Every seasoned and successful businessperson has had plenty of experience with deploying rapid, decisive action. My favorite example of the violence-of-action principle is the story of what my friend Amit Verma did with his parents' luxury jewelry company during the Great Recession.

Amit grew up in the jewelry and diamond business; his parents, first-generation Americans, had built a company, East West Jewelers, that was one of the most successful on Long Island.

In 2005, Amit had just graduated from college and started his own wholesale diamond business in Manhattan's diamond district, which was going fairly well. But his parents' business was taking on water and sinking fast. Long before the public felt the first major tremors of what was coming, it was already shaking the foundations at East West Jewelers.

"Luxury markets feel the financial crunch before anyone else," says Amit, "before the housing market, before anything else. By 2007 it was bad, and it got rapidly worse."

On top of the overall economic slowdown, a sudden explosion in gold prices exacerbated their problems. They might buy gold from an overseas supplier, say from India, at $1,000 an ounce, but gold prices were increasing so rapidly that before they knew it, the numbers might have gone up to $1,500, $1,600, even $1,700. They would take delivery of what they *thought* was $100,000 worth of merchandise, based on $1,000 an ounce, and take out a loan based on that. But as the price of gold skyrocketed, the price of that merchandise delivery would explode, so that while they *thought* they owed $100,000 on it, they now owed a great deal more. They would arrive at a figure for what the business owed, but every day it would increase—3 percent, 5 percent, 10 percent. Talk about being kicked when you were already down.

At first, Amit didn't realize how serious things were. Once he saw the extent of it, how many millions of dollars in debt they were, he and one of his brothers, Gaurav, stopped everything they were doing to jump on board with their business to see if they could help them recover and get back on track. By this time, the family business was close to $6 million in the red. They couldn't sell their way out of this. They had to do something radical. What they needed was violence of action.

At the time, they were starting to melt down some of their merchandise and resell it at a loss, just to generate enough income to pay their bills. If they took a piece of jewelry they'd paid $10 for, they might melt it down and get $6 for it. That meant right away they'd lost $4, but if that was the only income they could get, then they'd take the loss. To survive, you do what you have to do.

Then Amit had a thought. Instead of melting down their inventory of luxury goods, they could get their hands on some cheaper merchandise, then melt *that* down and resell it at a profit. Where could they get cheap merchandise? From the public.

Amit and Gaurav started haunting pawnshops, buying up everything they could. They started advertising: "We buy your gold!" They opened a storefront to sell their budget wares, and the plan was clearly working—but they soon realized that what they could do in this one location wouldn't be enough to get out of debt. So they opened up more storefronts. At the height of their operation, they would have nearly fifty stores running.

Amit vividly remembers preparing for their first public one-day buying event. He wanted to take out a full-page ad in *Newsday*, the Long Island newspaper, which cost something like $5,000 for a single day. He saved up for that $5,000 and did his ad: "Come Sell to Us." In that one-day event, they made back the cost of the ad, plus another five grand on top of that. As tempting as it was to pour that money into the business's pressing ongoing expenses, he immediately used it to take out *two* full-page ads for a second event. A few days later, he doubled it again. Before long, he was spending $25,000 in a day.

Of course, the capital investment involved in opening all these storefronts, along with all his advertising costs, was enormously risky. Everything they did was a gamble.

I imagine it felt a lot like jumping out an airplane in midair at twelve thousand feet.

Practically overnight, Amit and Gaurav had turned the family business completely upside down. From their highly respected, high-end luxury jewelry business, a family business they had built up over decades and were justly proud of, the Verma family was now suddenly the No. 1 pawnshop and "gold mine" business on Long Island.

Their parents were horrified.

Mr. Verma kept saying, "No, no, I don't want to do this!" Even as he saw the money starting to flow in, the idea of what they were doing was extremely upsetting to him. He and his wife had been the first to import 22-karat Indian gold jewelry into America; their business had been not only a powerful success but a powerful legacy. And now they were hawkers of WE BUY YOUR GOLD! print and TV ads! Because bright yellow seemed like the most glaringly obnoxious color they could come up with, Amit and Gaurav had painted their storefront yellow and plastered across the wall in giant capital letters the words WE BUY GOLD. His father was mortified. Customers lined up.

Amit saw an obnoxious television ad in Buffalo, with an announcer's voice saying, "We buy it, we buy it, we buy it . . ." over and over. It was quite annoying, but it stuck in your head. He contacted the guy who did the commercial and got his help making one for them. They started pouring money into more TV ads.

Friends and those who knew them started buzzing about them on social media: "What's going on with the Verma family? . . . I hear they've gone out of business . . . they have this weird ugly yellow building . . . what the heck are they doing?"

But to Amit and Gaurav, this was a simple question of survival. They were living on as little as they possibly could and pouring every penny they made back into the new operation. They didn't care how they were perceived. They wanted to keep the boat from sinking. Nobody who knew them understood what on earth they were doing or why. But what they were doing was digging themselves out of a $6 million hole—fast.

By 2009, when the economy tanked and the government was setting up Cash for Clunkers and all kinds of efforts to bail things out, the Verma brothers had lines outside all their stores. Because they'd taken such strong action, so fast, and so early, they were way ahead of the curve. While everyone around them was panicking, they were making money hand over fist.

They decided to take it on the road. They picked a city, made a hotel reservation, and ran an ad ahead of time:

WE HAVE A SPECIALIST WHO BUYS BIG DIAMONDS AND JEWELRY!
FOR TWO DAYS ONLY, WE HAVE *A MILLION DOLLARS TO SPEND*!!

"We always advertised that we had a million dollars to spend," says Amit. "Even if we didn't exactly have that much cash on hand, we always partnered with people who did and who could back us up if we needed it. As long as the deal was there, the money would be there, too."

They would arrive, rent the hotel's ballroom as their retail front for that one day, and jam. As always, it was a high-stakes gamble. On some trips, there'd be a line out the door. Sometimes it would be a dud. They did hundreds of these open houses, up and down the East Coast, from Jersey to Florida, renting out a hotel room in a different city every night.

"I hit it as hard as I could," says Amit. "When it's raining, you need to be out there with as big a bucket as you can find. You need to be out there catching the money while it's pouring."

You see what I mean? *Violence of action.*

Soon the Vermas began noticing that others on Long Island were catching on to what they were doing and jumping on the band-wagon. Competing shops began popping up. By the time the gold rush was at full boom, they had over 150 competitors.

This is where a cool head and a big view come into play. As I said, there are times in business when the smart thing to do is wait and watch. Amit and Gaurav knew these other shops were only there for the short run and that once there was no more big money to be made, they would dry up and blow away.

"We waited them out," says Amit. "Eventually, they went away."

It took a few years, but by 2013 the family business was out of debt and flush again. So what did Amit do? Changed the model again.

As the economy recovered, Amit and Gaurav went back to their father and said, "Okay, it's time to go back to our original business model. It's time to start selling high-end jewelry again."

Once again, their father balked. By this time, he had completely come around to his sons' point of view. In fact, he'd gotten to the place where he liked buying from the public, and the last thing he wanted to do was to turn everything upside down again. It took a while to convince him it was time to once again open up a high-end retail store, but eventually the boys prevailed.

The Vermas had built up an excellent customer base over their twenty-five years in business. All they really had to do was pick up the phone and say, "Hey, we have a shop," and people started showing up.

Amit says he started seeing kids he'd known as youngsters, children of past customers whom he remembered trailing alongside their parents in the shop, now coming in to buy engagement and wedding rings. Soon he bought one himself.

After taking a break to get his MBA and get married, Amit pulled one more violence-of-action move: he opened his own business combining the best of both worlds—using his buying-from-the-public model but with high-end luxury items. If you're a jeweler needing to liquidate an entire shop, or an individual wanting to sell a $100,000 watch or a $500,000 stone, the Verma Group will come out, appraise it, and buy it.

Today, Amit is doing the exact same thing he was doing in 2009 in cheap hotel ballrooms up and down the East Coast—only now he's doing it on a multimillion-dollar scale.

Chapter 4
EXCELLENCE MATTERS

❉ ❉ ❉

n the second half of 2012, something strange started happening at SOFREP. I say "strange," because it wasn't something I'd expected, planned, or intended, or even anything I saw coming. In fact, I didn't fully realize it was happening until it was already well under way.

We had started out that February writing pieces aimed purely at the Spec Ops community. After all, that was our mission. But by that fall, it was clear that this was not all we were doing. We were also writing about foreign policy, international developments, and other current events. Our identity was shifting; we were changing the core description of what we did. Organically and without our having planned it this way, SOFREP was becoming a hard news site.

In the business and leadership literature, you read constantly about how important it is to have your mission clearly defined, how you need to emblazon that on a sign and hang it on the wall and make sure everyone in your company knows what it is. Apple = "The computer for the rest of us." FedEx = "The world on time." Nike = "To bring inspiration and innovation to every athlete in the world."

And that's great, as far as it goes. But here's the dirty little secret of business missions: Sometimes you don't really *know* what the ultimate mission is when you start. Sometimes you don't find out until you've been at it for a while. In fact, this happens a lot more often than you'd think.

You start out with what you *think* the mission is. But it shifts and changes, and if you're paying attention, you follow. You pivot. Pierre Omidyar started his little online gig as a way to sell his girlfriend's collection of Pez dispensers. Once the thing was in motion, I think we can all agree, the eBay mission grew. ("A global marketplace where practically anyone can trade practically anything, enabling economic opportunity around the world.")

That's what happened to SOFREP. Before our first year was out, our mission had shifted. This wasn't a top-down change; it didn't come from me; it came from the writers. And it happened because we had a standard, and that standard led us where *it* wanted to go, not where I originally thought it was going.

That standard was *excellence*.

It started in August 2012, with the announcement of *No Easy Day*, that firsthand account of the bin Laden mission, which sparked some controversy about the whole idea of SEALs going public with details of the raid. On September 12, *Time* published a piece I wrote on the subject titled "A (Former) SEAL Speaks Out . . . About (Former) SEALs Speaking Out."

That same day, my best friend, Glen Doherty, was killed in the attack on the American consulate and CIA annex in Benghazi.

Benghazi changed my life. Glen was my closest friend in the

world. We'd been SEAL Team Three teammates, and we'd gone through Naval Special Warfare (SEAL) sniper school together as shooting partners, three months that forged a lifelong bond. My kids knew him as Uncle Glen. Losing him hurt worse than I had known anything could hurt. It also upped my own sense of commitment, to do my best to live up to the standard Glen set—not just as a SEAL, but as a human being.

Benghazi not only changed my life; it also changed SOFREP. Benghazi was the signal event that really thrust SOFREP into the news business, because it showed us the gaping hole that existed in the conventional civilian media and underlined the responsibility we felt to address that deficit.

If there is one defining characteristic of who Special Operators are and how they operate, it is *excellence.* Excellence means exactly what it says: you *excel.* Everything everyone else does, you strive to do better: faster, sooner, more efficiently, more effectively, more reliably, more consistently, and with greater results. You take on the job at hand and do it to the limit of human possibility—and then do it better than that.

What I saw in the latter half of 2012 was American media doing a mediocre job. And it pushed every SEAL button I had.

In the aftermath of Benghazi, the mainstream conversation went absolutely nuts. There was a presidential election happening, and the whole event became ridiculously politicized—on both sides of the aisle. What got lost in the noise was both facts and perspective: what actually happened, and what it actually meant or didn't mean. Once again, we were the first media outlet to provide a detailed account of the events of September 11 and 12, 2012, from credible sources. Over the following months, we published dozens of pieces that put accurate information and reasoned perspective in front of the public.

At the same time, SOFREP's cadre of writers was growing. Our writers are all vets, including Special Operators from every branch: not only SEALs, but Rangers, Delta, air force controllers, marine force recon and MARSOC operators, people with high-level intel backgrounds, CIA experience, every type and level of active-duty, in-the-trenches history you can think of, and every one of them had the same kind of top-tier standards of excellence. These men and women were watching what was happening in the news cycle, and they weren't liking it. Not just about Libya, but in all the trouble spots around the world, from the Middle East to Africa to Europe to Asia to right here in the United States, an awful lot of what was being written in the existing media was bullshit. And this was across the board: Fox News, MSNBC, CNN, the *New York Times*, the *Wall Street Journal*, everyone—too many people were writing about topics and events plainly without knowing what the hell they were talking about.

Our guys had operated on the ground in all these places and in many cases still had extensive active networks in place in these AOs (areas of operation) that enabled them to give the story to the American public straight, without any spin. They started writing op-ed pieces and commentary on what was showing up in the news. Soon SOFREP writers were offering pointed critiques of everything from the Veterans Administration debacle to Special Operations Command mismanagement to overall foreign policy.

At the same time, we were also breaking stories, beating other outlets to the punch with accounts that were not only more accurate and better sourced but also more timely.

We were the first to report the death of Chris Kyle, when he was murdered on a shooting range in Texas.

When another SEAL from the bin Laden raid, Robert O'Neill, claimed in an exclusive interview in a major newsmagazine that he was the shooter who put the lethal bullet into bin Laden, we outed the story for what it was: a publicity grab. There were numerous holes in O'Neill's account; we printed them.

We broke the news on the first transgender SEAL, Kristin Beck. We also broke the story on the first openly gay SEAL, Brett Jones, then did a follow-up on Jones's contract with the CIA and broke the story about the intense and flagrant discrimination against him in the CIA.

In June 2013, we were the first outlet to publish Ambassador Stevens's personal diary. In our piece, we included reproductions of the last five pages of his diary, written in his hand, including the final page, jotted down on September 11, 2012, with its chilling concluding line: "Never ending security threats . . ."—after which the diary went blank. (Yes, he actually put the dot-dot-dot at the end of that final entry.)

The stories kept happening, and we decided to take our original reporting to the next level. Rather than simply comment from where we were, why not put our guys on the ground in hot spots around the world? We started by deploying Jack Murphy, our editor in chief, to Syria, where he did a series in late 2014 and early 2015, including his report on the YPJ (Kurdish militia) female snipers. (His account of how he physically managed to get on location, let alone what he found when he got there, is well worth the read.)

Then Jack went to Iraq, and then we had Jamie Read in Somalia reporting on Boko Haram, Buck Clay in Ukraine and developments there, others in Iraq and Syria, and still others reporting on the southern borders of eastern Europe. We broke stories on the United States' supplying funds to rebels who are now ISIS. In 2016, Jack scored an exclusive sit-down interview with Syria's president, Bashar al-Assad.

The conventional media tend to get these things wrong, or they'll jump on a story without carefully vetting it first. A lot of news sites don't really know the difference between a Sunni and a Shia, or how Kurdistan works into the whole Iraq mix and the complicated landscape there, with the different ethnic and tribal backgrounds. But people like Jack and Buck—this stuff was their bread and butter when they were deployed there on active duty. That was exactly what they were trained to understand.

For example, we had one of our writers in Somalia when the media reported a "terrorist attack." What actually happened was that a local warlord blew up a competitor's place. It wasn't terrorism; it was business as usual, Somalia-style. This was a significant journalistic error. By reporting it as "terrorism," these other outlets were stoking the whole public fear machine, and stoking it falsely, based on an entirely faulty premise. We reported it straight, explaining what was really going on. This is one major reason we've gained so many new subscribers: we've built a strong track record of fact-based reporting without the slant or outside influence that seems to affect the reporting on so many other news sites.

We started SOFREP with a stated mission to provide information for the Spec Ops community. We could have doggedly stuck with that. Instead, we followed our growing journalistic instincts.

Our writers were seeing mediocrity in the media, and they wanted to respond with the same level of excellence they had adhered to in the military. They had something to say. I let them say it. Today if you go to SOFREP, you'll see our mission statement at the top of the page: "Trusted news and intelligence from Spec Ops veterans."

Excellence, Journalism, and Democracy

After the Stevens diary piece, the rest of the news media could no longer ignore us. Mainstream journalists started reaching out to us, trying to get us to give them our sources. Fortunately, Jack and I were savvy enough to realize that that would have been a very bad idea.

Even from the early days, we would often see reporters copying bits and pieces of our content in other outlets. We might do a really good story, say, about the Kurdish YPJ female snipers, and then a week later something would come out on that topic with very light sourcing; the author had obviously read it on SOFREP and tried to sort of make up his own story about it. We didn't have a problem with that, as long as authors would credit us and steer readers to our site.

Then one mainstream reporter lifted a story of ours, a story we'd broken just the day before, and showed up on CNN, reporting it and representing it as if he had broken this news himself. It was blatant.

Jeremy Scahill, the investigative reporter who wrote *Dirty Wars* and *Blackwater*, saw this happen and went public about it on Twitter. "This is wrong," he said (my paraphrase, not his exact words), "and you guys need to credit the original source." Scahill has a good-sized Twitter following. He shamed CNN into doing the right thing. The people at CNN didn't outright admit what they'd done, but they did credit us with breaking the story first.

Since then, I've gotten more than a few calls from major outlets, wanting to use a story we wrote and asking for our sources. Are they kidding? Give them our sources and let them claim the story as theirs?

No thanks.

Sometimes they'll then say, "Well, how about we contract you, and we'll give you credit."

And I say no, that's not the point. They're our sources. These are critical relationships we have, often with people in sensitive places. Do these outlets really think we're going to just turn over our sources to them? There's a level of arrogance there I find amazing.

As our new role unfolded, I also started getting a firsthand lesson in journalistic ethics and economics, and an eye-opening lesson it has been.

Editorial and advertising used to be separated from each other, like the wall between church and state. In today's digital world, with the acceleration of the 24/7 news cycle, media are more concerned with sensationalizing whatever trivial thing they can in order to get page views. Journalists are pressured by their content executives to drive page views, so they jump on a story, even if it isn't accurate, purely because it drives traffic. They're going to glom on, ride that train, punch up the headline, because each writer is under massive duress to deliver those clicks. When you have those economic incentives in place, journalistic integrity goes out the window. It turns into something like tabloid news, no better than the *National Enquirer*.

I understand that these media outlets operate with financial imperatives. I understand that they're a business. So is Hurricane Group. Of course we have to watch our bottom line, just like everyone else. As I mentioned in chapter 3, when we launch a new Web site, I typically give it six months to show enough growth and profitability to justify its existence. If the site can't make it on its own, even if I love the idea of keeping it open for the service it provides, we'll shut it down.

But you can't let economic imperatives control your editorial. And we don't. On SOFREP, Jack will cover something in the news purely because we think it should be covered. We know that nobody's going to be interested in reading about a thirteen-year-old American girl being kidnapped and trafficked through Morocco. We know most of our people don't want to read about that. But maybe, once you've put that piece out in the public eye, someone will put pressure on an elected official and get something done to change the situation. Maybe the spotlight will make a difference.

So yes, we'll do that kind of content, knowing that it's commercially irrelevant. I have to give due credit to the *New York Times* here, too; as much as it swings to the left, it also does a lot of good work like that, shining the light on things that need to be seen. It happens here and there in other outlets, too. But that kind of coverage is all too rare, and getting rarer by the month. More and more, what passes for "news" is driven by the dictates of generating as many page views as possible, which means it gets either sensationalized or politicized, or both. And when that happens, truth, accuracy, and perspective are left to bleed out on the battlefield.

The founders of this country knew that democracy works when there is an informed public. If the public doesn't know what the hell is going on and just runs with its emotions, then you've got mob rule, which may be the worst form of "government" there is. A responsibly informed public is the cornerstone of our way of life. And the only way you get that is with excellence in journalism.

Excellence matters.

Why Are You in Business?

It's no accident that *excellence* is principle No. 4—third from the front, third from the back, standing smack in the middle. Excellence is the keystone of the arch. Underlying all the other principles detailed in this book is a constant commitment to a standard of personal and professional greatness. Without that, none of the rest works.

If you don't hold an unreasonably high standard, then violence of action will just create a mess. If you aren't holding yourself to the highest standard, then your attempts to build total situational awareness will just become diffused attention and a scattered focus. And without uncompromising excellence, front sight focus is just putting on the blinders. Because, how do you know you're focusing on the right things?

When we were approaching the end of our work on *The Red Circle*, my writing partner, John Mann, and I started asking ourselves, why were we writing this book? Yes, I wanted to tell my story. But bottom line, what was the point? We decided to see if we could capture the essential message of the whole four-hundred-page book in the last page or two. Here's what we wrote:

I've thought long and hard about why I am writing this book and what I want it to say. I think the message I want my story to get across boils down to two words: *Excellence matters.*

Throughout my time with the navy and within the SEAL community, I've seen poor leadership and exceptional leadership. I've seen training that was simply good, training that was great, and training so transcendingly amazing it blew my mind. And I've seen the difference it makes.

In political matters I have always been a down-the-middle-line person. When it comes to leaders, I care less about their party affiliation and more about their character and competence. I don't care how they would vote on school prayer, or abortion, or gay marriage, or gun laws. I want to know that *they* know what the hell they're doing, and that they are made of that kind of unswerving steel that will not be rattled in moments that count, no matter what is coming at them. I want to know that they won't flinch in the face of debate, danger, or death.

I want to know that they excel at what they do.

A free society looks as if it rests on big principles and lofty ideals, and maybe it does for much of the time. But in the dark times, those times that count most, what it comes down to is not reason or rhetoric but pure commitment, honed over time into the fabric of excellence.

Why am I telling you this? Because it *matters.*

You may never shoot a sniper rifle. You may never serve as part of an assault team, or stand security in combat, or board a hostile ship at midnight on the high seas. You may never wear a uniform; hell, you may never even throw a punch in the name of freedom. I'll tell you what, though. Whatever it is that you do, you are making a stand, either for excellence or for mediocrity.

This is what I learned about being a Navy SEAL: it is all about excellence, and about never giving up on yourself. And that is the red circle I will continue to hold, no matter what.

That took 367 words, but really, you can compress it down to just two: "Excellence matters."

After the book came out, we got plenty of great reader comments, on Amazon and on social media. But far and away the thing we heard about most was those last two pages, and especially those two words. Ponder that for a moment: In order to tell my story of growing up and going through a decade of the SEAL experience, we used close to 135,000 words. And what people took away from it, more than anything else, was *two words*.

I share this because I want you to ask the same question about the business you're in as we did about our book: What is the point? Why are you in business?

I'm sure you'll have your own answer, and it will have to do with your own situation, your own interests and values and life experiences. You know your own *why*. But let me offer a few general observations about that question and its answer.

My belief is that the purpose of any outstandingly successful business is not to make money. The money's great, but that's not the point. The point is to *do* something great, something that blows people's minds, something that, yes, changes the world. Admit it. Nothing less will satisfy you. Am I right?

I thought so.

So we're not here to talk about "getting by" or "making ends meet." If that's your goal, put this book down right now and walk away. Because we're here to look at the ingredients of outstanding, world-changing success. We're here to talk about *excellence*.

A Thirst for Excellence

When I entered the military, I had a single goal in mind.

I'd like to say I joined up out of love for my country, an irresistible desire to serve, a drive to help right wrongs and bring peace to troubled times, and a sense of obligation to give back to our free society for all the incredible things it had put in my life. Except none of that would be true. To be clear, all those things did develop over time. I have a hell of a lot more appreciation today for this noble, generous-minded, and at times bizarre experiment called the United States than I did when I was a nineteen-year-old kid. Righting wrongs, serving the greater good, a sense of gratitude for the freedoms and opportunity so many of us take for granted? I'm in. But back then? No. Back then there was one and only one gravitational pull that sucked me into Naval Special Warfare: a thirst to be the best.

I'd heard the SEALs were the best. So I joined the navy—but I honestly had no interest in being in the navy per se. I wanted to be a SEAL.

I believe that you, reading these words right now, have the same bone-level attraction to excellence that I and most of my Spec Ops buddies do. If you didn't, you wouldn't have read this far. But—and it is a very big but—I also believe that is not a universal trait.

The desires for food and water, shelter, safety, sex, companionship, recognition . . . I recognize all these as universal. I don't think there is a person alive who doesn't want, in some fundamental way, to be happy and to feel that his or her being here on the planet makes a positive difference. We are all, even the saddest and most twisted individuals among us, heroes of our own stories.

But the thirst for excellence? I don't think that one is universal. Frankly, I believe a lot of people just don't care. Pretty good is good enough, and average will do. I say that not as an indictment but purely as an observation. If there were no average, if there were no frankly piss-poor, then there would be nothing against which to measure excellence. It's just the way the world is built. Like the spectrum of visible light, there is a spectrum of achievement, with plenty of people vibrating away, content as pigs in slop, at the lower frequencies.

But that's not where entrepreneurial success lies. Entrepreneurial success comes into existence at the purple and ultraviolet edges of the spectrum.

Like my friend Nick English.

Nick has been fascinated with intricate machinery all his life. From an early age, he and his big brother, Giles, learned all about the construction of devices, from clock assemblies to yachts to airplanes, from their father, Euan, a Ph.D. engineer and ex-RAF pilot. One day, when Nick was twenty-four, he and his father were flying a World War II–vintage Harvard in a practice run for an airshow, when their plane got hung up in an inverted spin and had to crashland. Nick broke thirty bones; his father was killed.

Upon recovering, Nick realized life was too short not to spend it doing what he loved. In partnership with Giles, he started Bremont Watch Company, built around their shared love of aviation and their dad's dedication to excellence. A few years later, Martin-Baker, perhaps the world's leading manufacturer of ejection seat and related aviation-safety equipment, approached Bremont with the idea of co-branding a watch that could withstand the most brutal of conditions. Nick and Giles developed the watch; Martin-Baker put it through its paces, strapped to ejection seat dummies and blown up and out, over and over—and it still functioned flawlessly. Since then, working with squadron after squadron, they've created custom-built watches for air forces all over the world. In the fifteen years since Bremont's founding, they have become the face of military aviation timepieces.

I know exactly what Nick was seeing when he stared into the heart of complex machines as a kid—and I know exactly what happened to him. He was seduced into a lifelong love affair with excellence. That's a passion I share, and I suspect you do, too.

Excellence lies at the heart of greatness.

Really, how great could a shoe company be? How excited could you get, could *anyone* get, about selling shoes? How much more boring could something be than the thermostat that controls the heat in your house? What sorts of business prospects would you see in a cup of coffee, the ultimate symbol of next to worthlessness, as in, "That and a quarter will buy you a cup of coffee"?

Answer: Zappos, Nest, Starbucks.

What do those three business home runs have in common? A thirst for excellence.

Excellence Is a State of Mind

There are people in business, just as in any field, who have an un-canny skill set that seems gifted to them by birth. Like Mozart, who played violin and piano like a virtuoso at the age of six and as an adult would compose multiple pieces in his head at the same time, these business virtuosos possess incredible innate abilities.

That's not me. Probably not you, either.

If you're not a born-brilliant deal maker, if you don't come from a family dynasty of business success stories, if you didn't enter this world with a native instinct for the boardroom and the marketplace, then how do you raise your game to the level of genuine excellence? The answer is actually pretty simple: *you decide to.* Excellence, more than anything else, is a decision, a choice, a commitment.

A state of mind.

When I started out in BUD/S, there was a guy I'd known from an earlier BUD/S-preparation course. Let's call him Lars. This guy might have been the most perfect, athletically built physical speci-men I've ever met. The dude could crush the most excruciating rou-tine of calisthenics as if he were swatting flies. Lars was a god.

In our first week of First Phase, he quit.

I saw this happen over and over: guys who could physically outper-form me and my teammates without breaking a sweat, men who had qualified for Olympic trials and been at the top of their game in pro sports, yet who threw in the towel, rang that brass bell, quit, and went home defeated, while we went on to become SEALs. It shocked and baffled me then, but I understand it now. Excellence is not about inborn talent or natural skills. Excellence is purely a state of mind. A decision.

During BUD/S, I also saw guys like my friend Chris Campbell. Chris was one of the smallest guys in our class, easygoing and unprepossessing, about as "ordinary" and as far from Lars on the spectrum of likely to excel as you could imagine. Yet while Lars quit, Chris not only sailed through BUD/S but ended up becoming an exceptional operator for a top-tier unit. (You know the one I mean.)

It doesn't matter what your background is. What matters is your commitment to be the best.

Not long ago, I was interviewed for a piece in the *Harvard Business Review* about how SEALs train for leadership excellence. As we got to talking about my management experience as course master for the SEAL sniper program, the interviewer asked what advice I might have for organizations that wanted to train to "good enough."

"Sorry," I said. "That's a question I'm not willing to answer. I can't go there. It's just not in my DNA." Why would I want to be part of an organization that aimed at "good enough"? Who gives a shit about "competent"?

Shortly after Eric and I implemented our program of mental management in the sniper course, a pair of students came to me before a test and said, "Realistically, Chief, what are you expecting us to do on this first test?"

I told them I expected them to shoot *perfect scores.*

This was crazy. Nobody shot perfect scores. Competent, yes; very good, possibly. But perfect? Didn't happen. But that's what I told them—because that's what I expected.

They shot 100, 100, 100, and 95. As close to perfect as anyone had ever seen.

We taught our students to put themselves into an excellence state of mind. To see winning and success as inevitable.

Of course, that kind of exceptional performance doesn't just happen because of your mental state. It also takes a tremendous amount of practice, refinement, and training. But practice and training alone won't deliver those results.

Any highly successful businessperson who tells you luck was not a factor in his or her success is lying. The good news is, you can create your own luck by working like hell—and cultivating a state of mind that expects and accepts only the best.

Hire the Best

SEALs have a saying for everything. "The only easy day was yesterday." "Everyone wants to be a frogman on Friday." "It pays to be a winner." "Pain is weakness leaving the body."

But my favorite may be this one: "You can't polish a turd."

Yes, people will grow in the job: they'll grow in experience and knowledge and ability. But you can't expect anyone to grow into a commitment to excellence if he's starting out at mediocre. It just doesn't work that way.

There's a great line in the film *Jerry Maguire,* when Dorothy (Renée Zellweger) is telling her sister why she thinks she's falling in love with Jerry (Tom Cruise): "I love him for the man he wants to be; I love him for the man he *almost is.*"

Don't do the Dorothy; don't hire employees for the team members they *almost are.* Don't hire mediocre talent. Hold the standard. Hire people who share your commitment to excellence.

Hire the best.

When you need to hire a lawyer, hire the best. When you need to hire a designer, a writer, a marketer, a customer service person, a CFO, hire the best.

Of course "hire the best" may mean hire *the best you can,* given your circumstances. Obviously, when you're starting out, you may not be able to afford the most expensive legal firm or ad agency. But that's not what I mean. What I mean is, set a standard, and hold it. *Hire the best* doesn't have to mean *spend the most money.* Excellence doesn't have to break the bank.

In our first year, I realized that if we were going to be creating a lot of original video content, we needed a videographer on staff. Not only that, we needed an *excellent* videographer on staff. At the time, I was living in Tahoe. It wasn't like New York City or Los Angeles or Chicago, where you can find first-rate talent on any block. Tahoe was not exactly a metropolis teeming with media talent. Plus, I didn't have the budget for a position that a major established big-city talent would have commanded anyway.

I went to the local college and asked, "Who's your best video student?" They pointed out a kid named Nick Cahill. I talked with him and brought him on, at first as an intern.

Good move.

Nick is an amazing talent. He loved the work, loved what we were doing, and rose to the occasion. He's now media director for Hurricane, and for a media company that's a pretty serious position. In 2015, one of Nick's photographs was selected for the cover of *National Geographic* magazine's special "Guide to the Night Sky" issue. Excellence doesn't come much better than that.

Improve Constantly

Strong leaders never ask their teams to do anything they aren't willing to do themselves. That's a core leadership principle we'll talk about more in chapter 7. The corollary is also true: as a strong leader, you need to hold your team to the same standard of excellence you hold yourself.

"Improve constantly" is a mantra that needs to be at the core of your company ethic, not just for you, but for everyone on the team, too.

In practice, this means you're always looking for ways to do it better, faster, stronger, to an even higher standard. Always pushing the envelope. Always asking those critical questions: How can we do this better? How can we take on bigger market share? How can we double our size—triple it, multiply it times ten?

In the SEALs, we not only train constantly; we also train harder than we expect to have to perform. When you study the great performers—in sports, the arts, business, or any other field—you'll always find they have undertaken massive amounts of training. And when that training is complete? Then they train some more, and harder than they expect to perform. Why? Training builds confidence and ensures peak performance. Under pressure, you don't rise to the occasion; you sink to the level of your training. That's why we train so hard.

Over the course of the seven months of BUD/S, we performed a huge range of brutally difficult tasks in all kinds of punishing environments (SEAL stands for sea, air, and land—in other words, the capacity to perform at maximum tolerances in *any* environment). But even with all those different disciplines and fiendishly difficult field conditions, BUD/S was really designed to teach us just one point: that we could perform far beyond what we thought were our limits. That most people are capable of ten times the output they have come to accept as "normal." Some absorbed that lesson; some didn't. Those who did went on to become SEALs. In business, those who learn that same lesson go on to achieve success at the top of their field, because they continually expect more from themselves.

Look at a Beethoven or a Picasso: they were constantly pushing themselves. The work they created late in their lives was nothing like what they'd done twenty or thirty years earlier. They never stopped exploring and stretching their own boundaries. That's what you have to do in business. Get better, smarter, clearer, more attuned. Become a better judge of character. Gain a larger perspective. If you are an excellent CEO, then I should be able to pluck you out of your current business and drop you in the CEO's chair of any major business in America, and within less than thirty days—hell, less than *ten* days—you should be not only running that business but already coming up with ways to improve it. Not because you know that particular business, but because you know how to learn.

What's more, excellence is contagious. It's your own drive for excellence that motivates not only you but also those around you. Great players want to be on great teams. If you want excellence in your team, they need to see it in you. Change has to start in you before you can expect it in others.

And then, expect it in them.

Never Settle

I've had friends in the Spec Ops community whose lives have essentially gone downhill ever since leaving the military. I understand that only too well. It's hard to fully describe the Spec Ops experience to anyone who hasn't been there: not only the training and exceptional level of performance, but also the sense of team and community, something that burns so deep it's hard to put into words. And it's easy to think, *I will never have anything like that again.* Once you've been part of such an intensely high-achievement community, it's natural to feel that nothing else you could possibly do will ever come close to equaling that experience. The way these guys see it, nothing in civilian life could even begin to compare with being a SEAL, or Delta, or Ranger, or whatever. In their worldview, the rest of life automatically pales. In a sense, their lives *had* to go downhill.

You don't have to be in Spec Ops to see this, or in the military at all. You've probably got friends who can't stop talking about their college football days, or about the old neighborhood, or about the way things were when they first joined the company as young pups. Blah blah blah. People have been torpedoing their own chances of success by their addictive attachment to the "good old days" forever.

There's a word for that point of view: "settling."

Fortunately, that's not what happens for most of us. The majority of guys I've known in Spec Ops refuse to accept that defeatist verdict, refuse to entertain the notion that the quality, juice, and excitement of our lives have to decline simply because we're no longer serving on the battlefield of war. Here in the civilian field, we have our own battle cry: "Never settle."

Refusing to settle often means you have to make hard choices. You'll find yourself in a situation where the present course of events is . . . acceptable. Reasonable enough. Not perfect, but pretty good. And who wants to risk rocking the boat, right? So what do you do?

Rock the boat.

When SOFREP Radio first took off, it was going so fast and doing so well that it would have been temptingly easy to overlook the fact that we had a real problem. Our on-air moderator, a guy who'd helped launch the idea, had some serious attitude issues and was starting to make a power grab, cutting out other team members in the process. I had to drop him. It wasn't fun and it wasn't pretty, but it was critically necessary. If I hadn't made the decision, SOFREP Radio would sooner or later have foundered and sunk.

In his place, I landed Ian Scotto, an outstanding talent who'd worked with Larry King and was currently doing a gig at Sirius XM with Andrew Wilkow. Ian has done every SOFREP Radio broadcast since that day. One of the best decisions I've ever made.

The book you hold in your hands was originally contracted to be published by a different publisher. Good people, and a good house, but they weren't really a *business* publisher, and their hearts weren't in it. At one point, we decided to pull out and look for a different home. We had to pay back the original advance (ouch) and delay publication (ouch again), and it was a royal pain in the ass for everyone involved. But we ended up placing the book at Portfolio, a company that in the business publishing world is excellence personified. Publishing partners don't get any better than this.

Sometimes it's better to rock the boat now than see it crash, or take on water and slowly sink later.

By the way, when I say "never settle," I don't mean that in legal terms. Any businessperson who claims "I never settle a lawsuit" is an idiot or a blowhard. Lawsuits, unfortunately, are a fact of life in modern business, and settling suits is sometimes both smart and necessary. Other times it isn't, because the other side is bluffing. I can't tell you which is which; that's why you need an excellent lawyer you trust.

There's a suit right now that my lawyers have urged me to file. Someone has violated the terms of an agreement, and I'm told I could easily win a hundred grand if I would just file. I'm not doing it. Life is too short, too sweet, and too precious to get entangled in that crap unless it's absolutely necessary. When it comes to lawsuits, I'm with Sun Tzu: the supreme art of war is to subdue the enemy without fighting.

"Never settle" also doesn't mean never compromise. Real life is full of compromise, and so is real business. This is something I've noticed former Spec Ops guys sometimes have a hard time learning. SEALs will go through brick walls; it's what we're trained to do. But you can't balls-and-bluster your way through a complex business negotiation. Good business takes sensitivity and nuance, not just supreme confidence and outstanding performance.

"Never settle" doesn't mean you become a bull in a china shop. It simply means this: you refuse to accept mediocrity. It blows my mind how many people will accept a half-assed job, in others and even in themselves, as "good enough." I have learned to be a patient man, but that is something I have no patience for.

Thomas Watson, the legendary CEO of IBM, gave this formula for achieving excellence: "As of this second, quit doing less than excellent work."

Pretty simple, isn't it?

Put Yourself in an Environment of Excellence

I mentioned earlier that I took a two-year business course, back in 2007 and 2008, when I was working on Wind Zero. It was my friend Randy Kelley (the same fellow SEAL who forced me to learn how to do my own numbers) who got me into that course. Modeled after the GE executive business school program, the course taught some MBA-level content, with some excellent psychology and philosophy thrown into the mix. During the program, they had us all read the book *The Tree of Knowledge: The Biological Roots of Human Understanding,* by Humberto Maturana and Francisco Varela. This is one heavy read, a book about cognition, neurology, and philosophical questions about perception—not the kind of book you'd expect in your garden-variety business course.

It had a huge impact on me. One of the things *Tree* talks about is how biological beings adapt to their surroundings, how organisms go through physical changes, changes in their biology and chemistry down to the cellular level, based on adaptation to their environment, and what the implications of all that are for how you and I learn and understand our world and adapt to our surroundings.

When I read this, a light went on. You have to surround yourself with the right environment, whether that means building that environment around you or moving yourself to where it already exists. If you want to perform at a certain level, you have to put yourself in an environment that exemplifies that level.

Five years after the course ended, I found myself thinking about Maturana and Varela's book again. A lot. SOFREP was growing like a weed, and I'd now started the Hurricane Group to contain all the other initiatives that were springing up. The business was becoming larger, more complex, and in many ways more challenging. I felt more and more responsible—to my growing staff, to our readership and customers. I needed to keep upping my game.

I wasn't living in the right place. When I started the business, I'd moved to Tahoe, which was secluded and peaceful. There was only one problem. It was secluded and peaceful.

I was flying to New York constantly to meet with publishers, do TV spots, or participate in some other media-related meeting. New York was the media capital of the country, the hub of all the activity I was increasingly involved with. I began to realize that running a media business and *not* being based in New York was like being in the film business and not living in Hollywood. Flying in for meetings, no matter how often I did it, wasn't going to cut it.

I had to *move* to New York. The media connections I needed would only happen if I were there.

Only in New York would I happen to make friends with Nick Ganju, the co-founder of Zocdoc, the massively successful medical portal company. Only in New York would I bump into Nick getting coffee and have him say, "Oh, hey, you want to meet Matt Meeker?" The guy who started BarkBox, the $200 million subscription box company? Yeah, I would love that introduction. And only in New York would I be having lunch with Matt a week later and end up forming a strong friendship and having him join our advisory board.

You'll meet Matt in chapter 7, "Lead from the Front." If I hadn't had lunch with him that day, he wouldn't be in this book.

If I hadn't moved to New York, I'm not sure this book would even exist.

I'm not saying you have to move to New York (media), or Hollywood (film), or Chicago (comedy), or Washington (politics), or Paris (cooking). My point is, whatever you want to excel at, you need to surround yourself with *that*, and more specifically with the *best* of that.

Upgrade Your Sphere of Friends

Over the past handful of years, I've come to have a great respect for the principle that excellence comes from the company you keep. (So does mediocrity, by the way.) You'd think I would have learned that principle through being a SEAL. And it's true, to an extent: being part of the SEAL teams was always about excellence. But it wasn't until I was out of the military altogether and going through my own learning curve in the civilian world of business that it started to sink in.

The SEAL experience provides a lot of powerful lessons, but it's an incomplete picture. I've seen a lot of guys come out of the Spec Ops world and go charging into business with this untempered sort of warrior mentality, and it doesn't work. The execution may be strong, but you can't just lash out at people when you meet resistance. You can't zip-tie, hood, and bag a noncompliant client.

I learned excellent success principles in the Spec Ops world, principles that apply beautifully to business. But that was only half my education. It was only when I started to hang out with master warriors in the field of business that I began to understand some of the finesse and nuance involved in applying those principles to the world of business.

When I got the acquisition offer from Scout Media in 2014, there were a few people I knew I could rely on for solid advice. But I knew I needed more than that. In former SEALs, like Randy Kelley, I had friends who were also accomplished in business. As a whole, though, my circle of SEAL friends was not going to take me where I needed to go in business.

I needed to enlarge my sphere of friends.

One of those I talked to at the time was Brian Margarita, a friend from San Diego who had subleased office space to me back when I was working on Wind Zero. Brian and I had become fast friends. He was also a member of a group called Entrepreneurs' Organization (EO) in San Diego. "But it has chapters in every state," he told me, "and for that matter all over the world."

He told me to go check out the New York chapter. I did, and it was one of the best pieces of advice I ever got. Joining EO introduced me instantly to a whole new group of friends in New York who were operating at a very high level. I'd tapped into a network of people I've since come to view as my Spec Ops buddies of the business world.

EO may not be the organization for you (to join, you must be the owner, founder, or majority stockholder of a business doing at least a million a year), but no matter who you are or where you are, there are organizations and networks that will put you in the midst of excellence. Reach out and swing for the fences. As I said, if you aspire to excellence in your performance, you need to surround yourself with an environment of excellence—and perhaps the most important environment of all is that created by the people you spend time with.

Embody Excellence

I mean this literally. If you want to produce excellence in your performance, then it's reasonable to expect that you need to *embody* excellence. That is, in your body.

You can't achieve your best if you're not in great shape yourself.

Given my background as a SEAL, you may be expecting that this is where we'll look at the type of insane, ball-busting regimen I recommend for extreme fitness. If so, you'll be disappointed. Training to take down a compound of armed insurgents in hostile territory in the middle of the night on the other side of the world is not the same thing as training to be a fit and productive businessperson. We're not going to go crazy here.

The diets and the fads and the masochistic workouts and the New Year's resolutions—it's all bullshit. It drives me crazy how people do these things in the name of fitness. There's a difference between fitness and intentional self-punishment. In the SEAL teams, we worked our bodies viciously hard, beyond tolerance. But let's remember the point of that: we were trying to protect our country from hostile forces bent on its destruction. It wasn't to get healthy; it wasn't because it was good for us. It was *terrible* for us. I wore my body out, starting with my back. I don't know a former SEAL who doesn't have profound joint issues, back or knee or hip, or some other irreversible damage. That wasn't a fitness plan; that was sacrifice for our country. It makes absolutely no sense for normal citizens to punish themselves that way.

I'm a strong believer in the impact of everyday lifestyle. You have to have a reasonable, healthy lifestyle and way of eating, something you can maintain in the course of your normal everyday life. You have to adapt your lifestyle to eating healthy and working out in a manageable way. Even if that's just walking. Walking is excellent.

I have a solid travel routine. If I'm on the road, say in Europe, I walk a lot, every chance I get. If it's a choice between taking a cab and walking, if it's practical, I'll walk. Every morning when I get up, I do a hundred crunches, fifty push-ups, and a bunch of yoga stretches. That gives me a physiological *and* psychological boost. I know I just got my exercise in, and I'm maintaining a basic minimum level of fitness. I go on hikes when I can.

It's not complicated. It's not an elaborate workout. If it's complicated, you won't do it. And you don't need complicated anyway. Life is complicated enough.

At a physical not long ago, my doctor told me that I'd gained thirty pounds. Damn. I was working out, swimming six or seven miles a week, eating good food—but I was eating too much.

I could have gone on a crash program to lose that weight fast . . . and then gone back and done it all over again. Instead, I said, *Hey, I've got to reduce my caloric intake.*

Now I eat a small breakfast, light lunch, and normal dinner. Nothing radical; just consistently a little less than I was eating. I incorporate activities when I can, like surfing and skiing, and I walk in the city as much as possible. I'll walk ten, fifteen miles a day in New York. I don't take cabs or subways unless I'm in a serious hurry. I lost the weight and haven't put it back on. I don't plan to.

That's sustainable. Unlike taking a pill, or going on a crash diet, or following some extreme workout program.

More than once, I've sat across the boardroom table from a guy who is making really bad decisions, and I can see his health is just crap. I can see it, because he's talking crap and thinking crap. No doubt, he's eating crap. I've met plenty of people who are making lots of money but are not fulfilled or happy. I attribute this to their not being well rounded, with a healthy family life, active hobbies or interests, and sound health of mind and body. Nothing you do is going to be the embodiment of excellence if *you* don't embody excellence yourself.

Strive for Excellence in Every Aspect of Your Life

Excellence matters in everything you do, not only in fitness, but in *everything*. The food you eat, the clothes you wear, the music you listen to. The shows and films you watch. The words and sentences you speak. The quality of your relationships. You should be a connoisseur of greatness.

I'm not saying your clothes have to be expensive or that you should be some stuck-up asshole putting on pretensions. Far from it. I'm saying you should bring those same standards of excellence you apply to your business into every corner of your life. You should be striving for excellence *everywhere*.

Again, how you do anything is how you do everything.

I think a taste for excellence is something you're born with. Maybe early childhood has something to do with it, too, I don't know, but in any case, by the time you've outgrown your acne and the early painful thrill of discovering you have hormones, either you have it or you don't. It's not something you can pick up in a continuing education class at the annex, and it sure as hell isn't something you can download.

You can *train* for it, though. You can hone it, sharpen it, and exercise it, and the more you do, the stronger and sharper and more deadly—that is, the more effective—it becomes.

Your commitment to excellence, or lack thereof, defines who you are as an individual. It dictates how you perform when everyone is watching, but it is also the standard you set for yourself when no one is looking. It's just how you do things.

You could call it pride in what you do.

When I was first back from Afghanistan, I was deployed as part of a small group called "sniper cell" to teach advanced sniper modules. One of the programs we taught was a rural training, where we would bring new sniper school graduates up to the Washington border near the Canadian wilderness to hunt elk and whitetail deer. While we were up there, we took turns making lunch for the group. Here we were, a bunch of trained killers out in the wild, and if you had watched us trying to outdo each other over the campfire and heard us arguing over who had the best recipe, you'd have thought it was a Food Network show. In those moments, we weren't snipers, hunters, or Spec Ops warriors; we were chefs, each doing our damnedest to out-excellent the others.

There are some things I've always had a feeling for, like athletics and extreme sports. Reading is another. I've always been a voracious reader, and being well-read, articulate, and informed is important to me.

But there are also areas where I've had to work at it. Give you an example: relationships. Some people are naturally gifted at getting along with others. I had to learn. I'm not natively a "people person."

When I was a kid, I got into a lot of fights. It's not that I'm insensitive or abrasive. It's just that being diplomatic is not my native language and I tend to be headstrong. But if I didn't start out being excellent in this area, or anywhere near excellent, it has been important to me that I learn to *be* excellent. And I've learned from the best.

Glen Doherty was the most naturally gifted people person I've ever known. Glen used to say he was there to run interference for me, to let people know that Brandon was a decent guy with good intentions, even if they'd had a run-in with me. We used to laugh about it, but there was a lot of truth to it.

It was impossible *not* to love Glen. He had more friends than anyone else I've ever known. That was no accident; he went out of his way to take care of those relationships. I had to learn from his example, and I have.

Joe Apfelbaum, whom you met in chapter 1, is another friend who is masterful at relationships. "The bigger your business," says Joe, "the more it depends on relationships. I take my relationships seriously and spend time on each and every relationship that I want to build. Our clients all came from building relationships with them one at a time and growing those relationships." I've learned from Joe, too.

It's not just that having better relationships serves the business. It's important for me to be a good friend—period. If I run a successful business and make a pile of money, but my health sucks, my friends are all pissed off at me, my kids don't know me, and I'm ignorant of the larger questions of life and musings of the world's great thinkers . . . then really, what's the point? If you're living a mediocre life and you get rich, all that extra money will buy is more mediocrity.

Excellence isn't simply a means to an end. It's a way of life.

Know That Excellence Comes at a Cost

A few years ago, I was at a serious low point (I'll say more about this and the reasons behind it in chapter 7), made worse by the fact that some disgruntled former members of the SEAL community were engaging in a smear campaign against me on social media and in the press. It was ugly, stupid, and pointless, but it was also a serious drain on my morale.

At the height of this episode, I happened to be out in California for a meeting with Mark Harmon, the actor and producer (best known for his work on the show *NCIS*).

I met Mark through Paradigm, the agency that represents us both. The people at the agency told me that when he was preparing for an episode of *NCIS* that involved snipers, Mark had read a book I wrote with my friend Glen, *Navy SEAL Sniper*. He loved the book, they said, and then read *The Red Circle* and loved that, too, and we met to talk about making a television show out of it. (As of this writing, that show is still in development with MGM; who knows, perhaps by the time you read these words, it will be airing.)

Mark, I soon learned, was also a huge aviation fan. During World War II, his father, Tom, had quite a storied career flying bombers. In April 1943, over South America en route to Africa, his plane broke up in a torrential storm, and the elder Harmon gave the order to bail out. He was the last one out of the plane, and he also turned out to be the sole survivor of the crash. Six months later, he was back in the sky again. He was later shot down by a Japanese Zero during a dogfight over China and was ultimately awarded a Purple Heart and a Silver Star.

And did I mention that before the war he won a Heisman Trophy and was inducted into the College Football Hall of Fame? If there was ever a guy who exemplified excellence, it was Tom Harmon.

Which made it all the more shocking to hear what Mark had to say.

When we met, I guess he could tell that something was bugging me, and I ended up telling him about the smear campaign that was dragging me down.

"Let me tell you something," he said.

He told me that back in the 1970s, when he (Mark, that is) was playing quarterback for UCLA, some guys came up to him and said, "Your dad's a freakin' coward, man."

His dad. Tom Harmon. The guy I just described. And they were saying he was a coward . . . because they'd heard something about how he bailed out of a plane and survived a crash when others died? Idiots.

Mark really looked up to his father, and hearing this was tough for him. And it wasn't just these guys this one time; the same thing happened to him repeatedly during those years.

"Here's the thing," Mark said. "You're always going to have people who are miserable in their own lives and just lash out, out of their own insecurities. And they always lash out at the brightest targets. It comes with the territory."

On one level, I already knew this, but in that moment it was incredibly helpful to hear. Especially from someone like Mark, who is not only one of the most successful television actors and producers around but also universally liked. Hollywood has its share of jerks and prima donnas, obviously. Then there are people like Tom Hanks and Ben Stiller, people who have reputations among their peers as being incredibly likable. Mark is like that: just a tremendous human being. Yet even *this* guy has to deal with his share of haters.

It felt comforting to have him share that experience, and to realize that I just have to be the best I can be and ignore all the bullshit that goes with it. You never see people who are happy with their lives exhibiting that kind of behavior. Successful people don't waste their time trying to tear down others—but they are often the targets of others who do.

That conversation with Mark taught me something: excellence comes at a cost. You know what, though? Mediocrity comes at a cost, too, and it's a much higher cost.

I'll take excellence.

PROFILE: SOLOMON CHOI
(16 HANDLES)

I met Solomon Choi through EO New York when he joined a forum in mid-2015 that I was moderating. We hit it off right away.

Sol's parents, like Amit Verma's, were first-generation immigrants who built a successful business here in the States. Where the Vermas built a high-end jewelry business on the East Coast, Mr. Choi found success as a multi-unit franchisee of a large Japanese seafood franchise, Todai Seafood Buffet, in Southern California. The family did well, and when Sol reached college age, his parents paid his way through four years of private school. Which only increased their horror when they saw what happened next.

Sol majored in marketing and planned on being a branding specialist, and it was no surprise when he received a job offer from one of the top consumer marketing firms in the country. But he had planned on traveling a little before starting work and had already booked a two-month tour of five countries in Southeast Asia. Could the company wait two months?

It could not. "Training starts in two weeks," Sol was told. "In Jacksonville, Florida."

So he turned the job down. And a bunch of others. In fact, the only job he could find that was willing to wait two months for his start date was as a rental agent behind a desk at Enterprise Rent-a-Car.

His classmates thought it was hilarious. His parents thought it was a catastrophe.

Sol loved it.

"At Enterprise," he says, "I learned the business practices and philosophy I still follow today: take care of the guests, take care of your people; growth and profits will follow."

No, it wasn't Avis or Hertz, but it was the company that kept winning J.D. Power and Associates awards for Best in Service, year after year. And at Enterprise he learned a pivotal principle about excellence.

"Renting cars is a commodity-based business," he explained. "Our cars were no different from what you'd get at Hertz or Avis; a Ford Taurus is a Ford Taurus. So why would a customer choose us over the competition, or even pay different rates for the same car?"

The answer was excellent service.

Enterprise was a very service-oriented organization. Your promotability was measured not only by your sales numbers but also by your ESQI scores: Enterprise Service Quality Index, based on phone surveys from your customers. Sol excelled at both. He moved up in the company and was soon managing his own satellite branch and did so well that he moved into Enterprise's sales department, where it sold cars it was taking out of service.

Imagine how his parents felt now: their college-educated son had graduated to the position of used-car salesman.

Still, they couldn't help being impressed at how well he did at it. Over the next six months, he won awards, trips to Hawaii and Catalina Island, and accolades from the company. At which point his mother approached him and said the family needed his help. His father's restaurant in San Diego was struggling. Competition had sprung up and taken away a significant amount of Mr. Choi's business. He didn't know what to do.

Sol was doing so well in business . . . could he help his parents?

If I say "Japanese restaurant," you probably think of something quaint and homey, a place that seats maybe fifty, sixty, even a hundred people. Not quite. With twenty-five thousand square feet and seating for five hundred, Todai San Diego was then the largest Asian restaurant in the United States. When Sol showed up, his first thought was, *This isn't a restaurant—this is a food factory!*

Sol had worked on and off at one of his dad's smaller Todai restaurants as a server and had some familiarity with the business but nothing from a management perspective. His father, who held a very traditional view about how the leadership track works, wanted Sol to spend two months as a dishwasher, then two months in line prep, then two months as a cook, and continue up the ladder until he eventually reached management. That's just how things were done.

Sol wasn't having any of that.

"Dad," he said, "if you want me to come help, I need to start as vice president of operations and marketing." His father laughed. Sol wasn't kidding. "Not only that, but you've got to allow me to make all marketing decisions, independently and on my own. I'll deal with corporate, and I'll deal with the franchisor. You have to let me general manage all of it—the whole thing."

His father didn't think Sol was ready for that.

"You have to trust me," said Sol. "If it doesn't work, you can go back to the way you were doing it, and I'll go back to Irvine and go on with my life."

His father agreed.

Sol met with the staff and told them that from this point on they were going to operate very differently, that they were going to engage differently with their guests and have a whole new level of attention to service.

He said, "I'm going to make you a promise. If you give me two months, I guarantee you will make more money, make better tips, and have more shifts. But you're going to have to work harder."

A third of the waitstaff quit. (Tells you something right there, doesn't it?)

Sol coached those who were left on how to create the kind of guest experience you'd find in a full-service, white-linen-tablecloth restaurant. Table-side manners, how to serve, how to pour wine, how to treat the guests—he took everything up a major notch. In two months, the average tip went from a dismal 7 percent to 13 percent—almost double, and close to industry standard.

The waitstaff were thrilled. Solomon, of course, wasn't satisfied. He wanted to keep raising the bar.

One day, poring over months and months of sales data, he realized there were three days in the year when they did significantly more business: Mother's Day, Father's Day, and Valentine's Day. On those three days, instead of having a lunch menu, then breaking down, resetting, and then opening again at 5:30 for dinner, they served one menu all day long. They not only stayed open all day; they essentially charged dinner prices all day. No wonder business surged on those days.

Sol started thinking: How could they make that even better? I mean, if you take your best day and make *that* better, what would that do to the other 364 days?

Mother's Day was coming. He researched all the other Mother's

Day buffets in the area to see what he was competing against. The local Marriott was charging $49.99. Sol wanted to charge $39.99—far more than the usual Todai price, but still well under the competition—but his father argued him down to $29.99. Given that budget, how could he improve the event? He ran the numbers and decided he could afford to include a bottle of inexpensive champagne (with plastic champagne flutes all around), a carnation for Mom, and king crab legs on the first display table (where guests would pass by while waiting in line on their way in) instead of the usual snow crab. He ran ads and put up posters announcing their "Super Seafood Menu." He wanted to make sure there was a waiting line all day long.

There was. When Mother's Day came, Sol worked the headset and hosted the whole day himself. He spoke with every single customer as they waited in line, in some cases up to forty minutes, telling them about what the restaurant was providing that day. He also talked to every single customer as they left, asking them how they'd enjoyed their meal.

They broke the company-wide record for sales in a single day.

"That's when I realized," he says, "that you can always find ways to do a superior job without breaking the bank. It comes down to attention—to quality, to service, and to execution."

A year later, his father sold the restaurant at a comfortable profit.

A few years later, Sol brought that same level of attention to excellence to the self-serve frozen yogurt business he created in New York, 16 Handles.

When he first arrived in the city, he spent two weeks walking around Manhattan to get a feel for all the neighborhoods. From Wall Street up past Times Square, everywhere. Finally, a real estate broker he was working with asked him what exactly he was looking for. Sol asked him, where did the NYU freshmen live? The broker took him to the largest freshman dorm in the East Village, on the corner of Third Ave and Tenth Street.

They walked around the neighborhood, and in a four-block radius Sol counted nine frozen yogurt shops. There was no other location in Manhattan with such an intense concentration of frozen yogurt shops.

"Perfect," said Sol. "I need a place right here."

His broker panicked. "No, no, no! You don't want to locate your shop here. That's crazy! Let me find you a nice spot in the Upper East Side or Midtown."

Sol insisted: he wanted to be right there. When the broker asked why, he said, "Because, if I can beat all nine of these shops, I'll be the No. 1 frozen dessert shop in New York City. Right?"

The broker looked at Sol as if he were nuts. "What makes you think you can beat all nine shops?"

Sol smiled. "Trust me."

He opened for business in his first location that summer, right there, on Second Avenue between Ninth and Tenth, on a Thursday. By that Saturday, he had a line out the door.

"The rest of that year was a blur," he says. "I worked almost every single day for months on end. I was *always* in the store." Obviously, it paid off. Of those nine competitors, eight have since shut down, and 16 Handles is the No. 1 frozen dessert shop in New York City.

So what did he do that the other nine shops—and all the other shops in New York City—didn't do?

For one thing, his flavors are better. From his restaurant experience in California, Sol knew which were the best flavors in the yogurt business. He approached vendors who were the top sellers back in California and secured distribution for New York.

"Nobody's been able to touch us on product," he says.

Not that they didn't try. Within a few years, copycat shops were starting to catch up. So Sol took another leap into excellence. In 2012, at the National Restaurant Association Show in Chicago, he met with an artisan creamery, a chef-driven operation that made handcrafted product in the Midwest using only local, all-natural ingredients in small batches. It was not making frozen yogurt at the time, only gelato, but Sol started working with the creamery on developing flavors for his frozen yogurt. In 2013, 16 Handles came out with a new proprietary line of flavors it called its artisan line.

For example, its So Fresh Mango Sorbetto is made from pureed tree-ripened mangoes from India, which Sol traveled to India himself to sample. "I've never tasted anything that sweet before." He has a team of chefs—not food chemists in lab coats trying to engineer flavors with chemicals, but actual chefs—creating the next new flavor sensation.

But it goes beyond the flavors. Sol did everything at a higher level of quality. "We wanted to be the Saks Fifth Avenue, the Whole Foods, the premier, luxury brand in our category," he says. And that's exactly what 16 Handles has done. Its store interiors are nicer than its competitors'. There's more engagement and attention to service. It has won awards for its ad campaigns and digital marketing (and has been a featured location in the HBO series *Girls*). From the recyclable spoons and biodegradable cups to its comfortable, loungelike ambience to its community engagement and attention to social media, Sol's enterprise (pun intended) is the embodiment of excellence and attention to quality.

Now he's taking that concept around the world. When I last talked to him, he had a total of forty 16 Handles stores in six states in the Northeast—all opened by former customers—and had just opened his first three stores in the Middle East.

I'm looking forward to an organic mango sorbetto next time I'm in Qatar.

Chapter 5
EMBRACE THE SUCK

❉ ❉ ❉

Webb, you are a worthless piece of shit! You've got no balls! You've got no spine! You've got no character! Do you even have the brains to realize what a worthless piece of shit you are?"

It is near the end of First Phase, just a few days before Hell Week. I am alone on the beach, surrounded by four BUD/S instructors goading me through hundreds of calisthenics, yelling at me at the top of their lungs, shoveling sand in my face, hurling insults, pushing as hard as they can. I am a wounded buck, surrounded by a pack of hyenas, a gazelle cornered by a pride of the veld's hungriest lions.

It is the lowest moment of my life. At least, up to this point. (There would be worse, but we'll get to that shortly.)

When I first checked into BUD/S, I thought I was in pretty good shape. It didn't take twenty-four hours to realize that in terms of fitness I am pretty much at the bottom of my class. Being one of the worst out of 220 guys: not a good feeling. And I am not a brand-new recruit; I've been in the navy already for more than four years and am an E-5, a senior guy, so everyone expects even more from me. It's a tough pill for my ego to swallow.

And there's nothing I can do about it but put my head down and suck it up.

At first, the other guys in my class would say, "C'mon, Webb, get your shit together." Now it's gotten to the point where I always get extra attention, no matter what. At room inspection every weekend, our room gets trashed by the instructors no matter how clean it is, purely because I'm here. Which doesn't make my roommates too happy with me. Nobody is too happy with me. The whole class is suffering because of me. It sucks to know that you are *that guy*. I don't blame people for wanting to steer clear of me; they don't want extra attention on themselves. Still, it's a lonely place to be.

Now, just a few days before Hell Week, it's all come to a head. The instructors have decided I don't belong here, and they're doing their level best to get rid of me. Not a few days from now, during Hell Week. Now.

To be fair to them, that's basically the staff's job in First Phase: weed out everyone at the low end of the curve so you lay a foundation for developing actual SEALs. That's how BUD/S is structured. Second Phase and Third Phase are for sorting out who has the intelligence and dexterity to deal with diving, shooting, handling explosives, and all the rest. First Phase is to flush out whoever doesn't even qualify to try. Those Second and Third Phase instructors are counting on the First Phase guys to thin the herd.

That's what is happening right now. I am the weak one, the one they are supposed to finish off and eat.

And they've got me. I'm at such a low point, not only physically exhausted but also beaten to shreds emotionally. I grew up in the Canadian wilderness, on a cattle ranch with no electricity or running water, but I've never felt such intense loneliness as I feel right now on this San Diego beach.

"Just quit, Webb! Why are you still here? You got nothing! You're a disgrace! You're garbage! You know damn well you're dragging down the rest of the team and everyone is praying you'll quit! For once be a man; just ring the damn bell and get it over with!"

They're right. There is nothing left in me . . . nothing except this: *I will not quit.*

You may call it an epiphany. For me, it's just a moment of recognizing the obvious. Lying here belly down on the sand, I suddenly see what is right in front of my face: *I am still here.*

Am I miserable? Totally. Does it suck? Copy that. Am I hating every second of what is happening? Affirmative.

So what?

I've already been through the worst they can throw at me. *I am still here.* They can kill me, but they can't make me quit.

I look up at one of the instructors, the one taking the alpha role in this beat-down, stare him in the eye, and croak, "The only way you're getting me out of here is in a body bag."

They send me back to my crew, and from this moment on they back off. I never hold my team back again. Over the next few months, I go from being at or near the bottom of my class to being one of the fewer than 10 percent who makes it all the way through BUD/S. From being one of the worst to being one of the best. And here's the point: It isn't that I've suddenly gotten that much stronger, or that much better, or that much more athletic. The only thing that changed, that afternoon on the beach, was that I made the decision to stay in the game no matter what.

I've decided to *embrace the suck*.

There's Gold Within the Muck

We have a saying in the SEAL teams: "It pays to be a winner." True enough—but one of the secrets to winning is embracing failures, obstacles, and losses. We have another saying: "The best ideas come from the worst places." Most outrageously successful business ideas are born out of the experience of failure, sometimes even bitter failure. The pain is temporary; the learning is priceless.

I thought about that day on the beach again more than a decade later as I sat in my car with my phone in my hand, gazing out over the cliffs of La Jolla at the Pacific Ocean. I'd thought that day in BUD/S was the lowest moment in my life. I shook my head and took a long, slow breath. Not true. This was lower.

I touched on this time briefly, earlier in this book, in telling you about my meeting with Todd Dakarmen. But that was a glossy, upbeat version of the story. Now that we know each other better, let me walk you through what it was really like.

I'd been out of the service now for five years. For most of that time, I'd been working on my multimillion-dollar brainchild in the Southern California desert. I'd poured all of myself into Wind Zero. I'd also poured about $4 million into it, much of that raised from investors, including friends, former SEAL teammates, even close family members. Everyone who believed in me. And it was all crashing down around me, smothered in a series of frivolous but suffocating environmental-impact lawsuits that I could no longer afford to fight.

The phone call I was about to make was to my lawyer, telling him to pull the plug. Four million, gone. Family, friends, the faith of dozens. Five years of my life. And that most precious asset of all, reputation—that house that, once you burn it down, is a bitch to rebuild.

I wanted to do what I'd done on that beach. I wanted to fix this thing with a cold stare and say, *Screw you, I'm not quitting, you'll have to take me out in a body bag.* But this wasn't BUD/S. This was business, and I was already in a body bag. My good friend John Tishler, who was also my lawyer, had confirmed it for me. "I see this kind of thing all the time, Brandon," he'd said. "It's at the point where you can't retrieve it. You have to let it go." I knew he was right.

I made the phone call.

Then things got even worse. The county was attempting to pierce the corporate veil and sue me personally. A couple of partners turned on me and sued me. I had to pay out close to a hundred grand—a hundred grand I didn't have—to settle debts that the company owed, obligations I'd taken on personally just to get the thing over with and move on with my life.

And then my wife let me know she couldn't stick out the marriage anymore.

The school year was about to start, and she didn't want to register the kids in one place, only to move them shortly thereafter, so the split had to happen right away. We had just moved into a brand-new rental, a really nice house with an ocean view, got a great deal on it. We had unpacked only a few days earlier. But it had to be now.

The day we broke it to the kids that we were separating was one of the worst days of my life. We'd gotten some excellent counseling and coaching with a local psychologist (the good ones are worth the money) on the best way to do this terrible thing, and to this day I'm grateful that we did; though it's hard to believe, I imagine it could have been even worse than it was. We took the kids to a random park, a place we'd never been to and none of them cared about, because we didn't want to burn this day in their memory in association with a place they loved. We sat them down and told them together. They were incredibly sad, of course. I cried like a little kid myself. It was brutal.

Give me four BUD/S instructors shoveling sand in my face over this, anytime. Hell, make it forty instructors.

Overnight—literally—I went from coaching Little League to living in an empty house, alone, no kids, nothing but a lot of uncomfortable conversations with my new neighbors. The phrase "low point" doesn't even touch the surface.

So, now what?

I could turn tail and leave the country: pack it in, move to Mexico, put my feet up, and spend my days eking out a lazy existence on my meager veterans' benefits. I know that sounds depressing as hell, but don't think the thought didn't cross my mind. But that would've meant walking away from my kids: not an option. Also, it smelled too much like the word "quit."

Or I could go the other way and reenlist in the navy. That thought crossed my mind, too, but in a way that also felt like quitting. That chapter of my life was behind me. I was supposed to be moving ahead, not moving backward.

Embrace the suck, I told myself.

I stayed.

Once I'd made that decision, it didn't take long to get back up, dust myself off, and start walking again. I took a nine-to-five job as an executive for a defense firm in San Diego, which I hated but it paid the bills. I broke the lease on the new place and moved in with a friend; once I was on my feet I found a smaller place just for myself.

Then something really interesting happened.

A few years earlier, when I was pushing hard on Wind Zero, a Web site sprang up protesting our project. Apparently, there was a groundswell of opposition from the community. I say "apparently" because it was all a smoke screen; turned out, the community had nothing to do with it. The whole thing was fabricated by a jealous former SEAL who considered himself my rival.

Soon after the "community protest" site went up, an anti-Brandon video showed up online, cobbling together bits and pieces of sound bites from interviews I'd done, all stitched together to make it sound as if I'd said things that I hadn't actually said at all. No surprise: it was that same ex-SEAL, playing a card from the politician's election-cycle dirty tricks deck.

The project was already struggling; having this noise mucking up the situation only made things worse. I had to do something. But I had no idea what. A friend told me how these things work: I couldn't get this crap taken down, he said, but what I *could* do was push it off the first page of search results by putting up a whole lot more content related to my name.

So I did. I started churning out content—releases, short articles, mini-essays, anything I could think of to push that ridiculous smear material off the first page. In the process, I discovered that I really enjoyed writing. A lot.

Now, a few years later, standing in the dust of Wind Zero and the ashes of my life as I'd known it, that discovery became my life-line. Writing and posting material online, which I had started doing purely as a tactic to survive a PR shitstorm, became the foundation of an idea I sketched out for a friend on the back of a napkin one day: a Web site devoted to Special Operations content.

It's not a stretch to say that if that Wind Zero smear campaign hadn't happened, there'd be no Hurricane Group today.

There's a reason this chapter is called "Embrace the Suck," and not simply "Survive" or "Outlast" the suck. Because it's not just a question of toughing it out or managing to get through it. You get to a point where you actually welcome it. It's not that you like it when these terrible situations present themselves. They bother me as much as they do anyone. It's that, once you pry them open, they contain gold.

Back when that online smear campaign first appeared, it would have been easy to say, "If it weren't for what these guys are doing, my business would be moving forward." In retrospect, though, I can see that the business was going to be destroyed anyway. I had no way of knowing that at the time. I had no way of knowing that the very thing that looked like my worst enemy was in fact planting the seed for my eventual success. But that's exactly the point. You *never* know those details at the time. You *never* know how this thing is going to work out five years from now. You *can't* know.

You'll find out soon enough. Right now, all you can do is embrace the suck.

Make Adversity Your Friend

It amazes me how many people in important business positions are so risk averse. I see them making decisions, or in some cases scrambling *not* to make decisions, strictly out of the desire to avoid pain and suffering. But if you do that, you also avoid those opportunities that come with adversity. You lose out on the gold. A genuine commitment to excellence is impossible without a deep appreciation of pain and failure.

The truth is, bad breaks, unexpected breakdowns, unfair kicks in the face? They offer you the best shot you have at taking your performance to the next level. World records aren't broken in practice; competitive environments and adversity are the birthplace of champions. Great leaders know that adversity produces the greatest opportunities.

Unexpected challenges may turn out to be your best shot at success.

In fact, often they are your *only* shot.

A great example of adversity in business is unexpected competition. If you make adversity your friend, then you start seeing competition not as the enemy but as an opportunity to challenge yourself and your organization, to learn, to adapt, and to exceed whatever level of performance you've taken as the maximum up to this point.

Problems are priceless. They clarify what it is you truly want. They push you to identify your passions and pursue them.

The word "no" doesn't exist for me. I hear people say it, but to me that's just the sound of the world giving me interesting feedback.

Nineteen people in twenty will tell you that you can't do the thing you're looking to do. What they really mean is, *they* can't do it. And they're right. But you can, and the obstacles that get in your way are only there to help you prove it. Obstacles are there to show how bad you want it and to force you into developing the skills and resources you need to get it. Treat every rejection, refusal, and reaction as currency you can use to purchase the motivation and endurance you'll need. Don't let the naysayers and the conventional-minded determine your future. That's your job, not theirs.

Invite criticism. Criticism is an excellent tool. Be honest and candid, and expect the same back. It can be more uncomfortable to seek out criticism than to avoid it—but it can also save your life. The day you stop getting criticism is the day you should start to worry. When people don't tell you what you're doing wrong, it means they've given up on you.

Don't React—Adapt and Thrive

One day in the summer of 2013, I was sitting in a boardroom in Texas, meeting with one of our major advertisers. Reps from its ad agency were there with us, too. There were some new people at the table, people we hadn't met before. As the conversation came around to editorial, I talked about how we were raising the bar on doing genuine reporting and breaking news, rather than focusing only on Spec Ops insider news and information.

As an example, I told them about a piece we had recently run on the first transgender Navy SEAL. His name (*his* when he was on active duty) was Chris Beck; now she was Kristin Beck. We were the first to break that story, and I was proud of it. (Still am.) I pointed out that mainstream media outlets were taking notice in a big way. CNN had reached out to us because of it, and others were coming to us, too, which in turn was upping our circulation as well as adding value to our brand and reputation. This client was, in other words, investing in a winner here.

The meeting broke, and I hopped a cab to the airport. As I waited to board my plane back to Lake Tahoe, where I was still living, my phone buzzed: an e-mail from the agency.

The message said, "Pull everything." The people from the agency, *the people I'd just met with,* wanted all their ads taken down, effective immediately.

To say I was angry understates it by a continent. I was royally, titanically pissed off. And this was not a matter of principle alone. It was also one of survival. We only had a few big sponsors at this point. These guys represented a million dollars a year in advertising to us, and it was terrifying to be so at the mercy of this one source, to be relying so heavily on one big customer that could just turn off the spigot like that.

We had some pretty heated exchanges with the ad agency, and I suspect they eventually realized that what they were doing—canceling all their ads purely because we'd run a story about a transgender SEAL—was discriminatory, especially once the mainstream outlets all started following the story, too. They turned it all back on again. But it was a hell of a scare, and it taught me something: we could not afford to be so vulnerable to a single revenue source. I didn't ever want to allow an advertiser to become so big and powerful that they would think they could bully us into not doing what we were there to do, which was to write and report on important topics.

I decided it was time to change our model. We would take SOF-REP to paid subscription.

On August 1, I posted this notice on the site:

Hi, Everyone—Rumor has it that SOFREP is going to switch to a paid membership in order to access the Web site. Rumor is right.

The main reason SOFREP.com is going to a membership model is to ensure the integrity of our content. Period. This move will also let us add more contributing editors to the site and continue to pay them for their work.

Back to the content part. We've had some amazing sponsors who are behind us 100 percent, but some sponsors would have us stay away from breaking stories and edgy topics. They want access to our community (us, you, and the active-duty audience), but only on their terms. War is not boring, and neither is our site—and we've got news for them: Special Ops don't work this way. Jack Murphy and I don't compromise when it comes to the integrity of this Web site, our content, or the community we've built with your help.

"You have enemies? Good. That means you've stood up for something, sometime in your life."—Winston Churchill

This was not an easy decision. I knew that making a move like this was incredibly risky. I felt sure that our offer of original content on SOFREP was strong enough to bring a lot of our readers along with the new plan. But still, it was a crapshoot. If all our readers bailed on us and nobody was willing to pay the fee, it could sink us.

Sure enough, we heard some howls of protest when I made the announcement. There were quite a few people who were unhappy with us. The first few weeks were a little bit like watching a hostile ship seize-and-search operation from a helo: sitting up in the bird as overwatch, eyes glued to the IR (infrared) monitor while your buddies below you swarm silently over the bad guys' ship, snaking up and over the rails and fanning out to take down the entire unsuspecting crew . . . This felt eerily similar: sitting there watching it unfold, and all you can really do is watch the monitor. It was unnerving. But by the time we were sixty days out from launching the new model, we had a few thousand subscribers, and I knew we were on solid ground. This was going to work.

And here is the gold within the muck: subscriptions turned out to provide a far more stable, reliable revenue stream than we'd ever had before. The fact was, advertising had always been fairly volatile for us; we never knew when we might lose a big advertiser and have to suddenly cut back on writer fees and let some writers go. Now the stability that our growing subscriber base provided allowed Jack and me to hire more writers and maintain a more stable writing team, which led to an uptick in the quality and consistency of our content.

That wasn't all. Over the next two years, Facebook started tightening up its guidelines on the advertising and sale of firearms through its ads, which threw the entire tactical industry into a tailspin. Of course we had advertisers who had nothing to do with that industry, companies like Apple, GM, Sony Pictures, St. Martin's Press, and Universal. But we also had a lot of advertisers who were affected. Which meant that those sites that relied on those advertisers were suddenly in a panic.

Not us.

In our first two years of business, advertising had represented about 90 percent of our revenue. By 2015, it represented no more than 25 percent; the rest was all membership. And that initial crisis, our biggest advertiser pulling out on us over the Kristin Beck article? Turned out to be a godsend. It may just have saved our lives.

That was the gold within the suck.

There's a postscript to the story, because as I was writing this chapter, we just had another major advertiser do the same thing.

Jack recently wrote a piece exposing something that this particular advertiser didn't like being written about, and they flipped out on us. We had a big conference call with them and their ad agency. They said that what we wrote was unsubstantiated crap and should never have been published, and they were reconsidering their ad commitment.

"How can we justify spending money with you guys," they said, "if you're going to write articles like this?"

Maybe they thought we would back right down because they were an important client of ours. Not a chance. I pushed back hard.

"Look," I said, "there are gonna be times when we write stuff you won't be happy with. That's just the way it is. There's nothing you can do about that. That's how journalism works. But here's what I'll promise you: if we made a mistake, if we were wrong in our facts, then we'll fix it.

"But in any case," I added, "you don't get to call the shots on our editorial content. You have zero say there. Just to be clear."

As it turned out, *they* were wrong. Jack showed them evidence he hadn't published that supported his position, and they had to concede that our article was accurate. Either way, though, they did not have us over a barrel, as they expected to. We were 100 percent prepared to walk away from them as a client. We had created a system of recurring reader-based revenue that made us invulnerable to advertiser pressure—and I made sure they knew that.

Rather than reacting, we adapted—and as a result we thrived.

Take It One Piece at a Time

Going through the stress of SEAL training and then sniper school taught me how to maintain my cool when dealing with difficult customers, vendors, and legal matters. In the sniper course, my fellow cadre and I created hundreds of high-pressure situations to make or break our sniper students, like the edge shot exercise I described in chapter 1.

As a CEO, I've found it a gift to know how to remain calm under corporate fire. It has also helped me model behavior for the rest of my team. They know I expect cool heads during stressful times, because they've seen it from me over and over—most recently, in the early months of 2016.

One of the Web sites in our network was being run by a friend who wanted out and had turned ownership over to another guy. I had now inherited a business partner I'd never had the chance to vet, and he turned out to be kind of a bull in a china shop. He started barking at my team and throwing his weight around. I told him he really had to curb that behavior. He got nasty and threatened to sue me. It got messy.

At the same time, a totally unrelated issue blew up. Someone I'd known in the past came out of the woodwork and threatened to sue over something that amounted to nothing.

So now I was dealing with the barking Web site guy's lawyer and the pissed-off guy from the past's lawyer, along with all the normal day-to-day craziness that goes with the business. For a few weeks there, everything was happening at once. My heart rate was elevated. I was genuinely stressed.

Finally, I had to take myself by the hand and say, "Okay, just *stop*. Take a deep breath. You know what to do here."

And I did. One of the most valuable things I learned in BUD/S was this: *Take it all one piece at a time*. If you look at everything coming at you all at once, it can seem overwhelming. But if you break it down into small pieces and take it a piece at a time, it eventually gets manageable. Take your pick: divorce, losing a loved one, losing a business or a job, whatever it is, you can get through it if you just take it in small bites.

First, I asked a mutual friend of the pissed-off dude from the past if he would meet with the guy and talk some sense into him. He agreed to do that.

While that was happening, I sat down and talked to the guy who was running the Web site. I got him off his ledge, walked him back from filing a suit, and was able to extricate him from the business.

There will always be times when the stress level gets insanely high, simply because there will always be things that go insanely—and unexpectedly—wrong. And typically major problems don't show up all by themselves, one at a time. It'd be nice if things worked that way, but they don't. This is real life, and it'll throw two, three, four major hassles at you all at once, just to see how you cope with it.

It's so easy to let that stress bleed out into your dealings with other people. I see people who can't keep their cool, blowing up at someone over e-mail. Which often blows up in their face, creating even more stress. You can't let your emotions get the best of you. You have to stay calm, even under pressure. *Especially* under pressure.

When life throws everything at you all at once, take control: take things one piece at a time.

Look for Clarity from the Crisis

One of the beauties of a crisis is that it can be a clarifying force, if instead of simply reacting, you use it as an opportunity to learn more about what's really going on.

I recently worked on a major advertising campaign for an important client. Their ad agency, who was coordinating the campaign, had historically been extremely difficult to work with, and they confirmed that track record once again: smack in the middle of executing on a branded video project, one of their young reps decided to cancel the campaign, even though it involved a significant amount of video production that had already been shot. My team had spent a lot of time and money producing this project; I had just returned from shooting with them in Europe when I got the news.

I had every reason to give this young agency rep a lesson in contracting and business ethics. As much as I would have loved to lay into him, I kept my cool on the call and didn't say much. After hanging up, I considered the situation. What were my options?

a. I could have my lawyer send a letter demanding payment for the canceled work. They would have had to pay. Still, I've never found this route to be a good idea in business; or

b. I could just tough it out, eat the loss, and try to work through an already difficult agency relationship; or

c. I could use this problem as an opportunity to bypass the agency altogether and potentially build a stronger relationship with my client.

I chose option *c*. On my dime, I flew out to our client's corporate headquarters and met directly with their digital team. I laid out the situation for them and was completely honest; I let them know that while we loved their brand and our relationship with them, we were prepared to walk from the business if their agency didn't start treating us as a partner.

It worked. The customer had no idea these problems were ongoing, and when they followed up, they discovered that other partners were experiencing similar issues. The client was grateful and committed to put top-down pressure on their advertising agency to do right by us. Today they are one of our biggest clients, and we have a fantastic relationship with them, regardless of what agency they work with, now or in the future.

A six-figure problem had turned into a seven-figure opportunity.

PROFILE: KAMAL RAVIKANT (*LOVE YOURSELF LIKE YOUR LIFE DEPENDS ON IT*)

For this chapter's profile, I didn't have to think long about who in my life knows all about embracing the suck. Kamal's name jumped up all by itself. It's not that the suck in his life has been so much worse than anyone else's. It's what he's *done* with the suck that makes him a natural for this topic.

Kamal joined the army at eighteen after a year of college and served as an 11 Bravo (infantry soldier) in the Tenth Mountain Division. After the army, he did trauma research in upstate New York emergency departments while attending courses at the University of Rochester, with the intention of becoming an emergency physician. Instead, he ended up moving to Silicon Valley, where he helped build a company named Healtheon, which became WebMD about the time of the dot-com boom. By the time Kamal left WebMD, he was running its home page. This was a big deal. If you were the guy in charge of the home page, you were one of the most important people there. At this point, it's safe to say that Kamal was hot stuff in the tech business world.

He briefly did some consulting for the pharmaceutical industry, which paid well, but it didn't take long to realize, as he puts it, "how that sucked my soul." He split and spent some time traveling—hiked the Himalayas and meditated with Tibetan monks, trekked 550 miles across Spain with Hemingway paperbacks in his back pocket, spent some time living in Paris. Eventually, he returned to Silicon Valley, where he started to work with tech companies again, even starting a few himself.

Meanwhile, Kamal was also moonlighting as an aspiring writer. He had a passion for writing and had been working away at it throughout his adventures. He didn't just read Hemingway while on his world travels; he read him over and over, poring through the prose like a World War II code breaker, reverse-engineering every paragraph, every line, every phrase, trying to understand how Papa did it.

The whole time he was writing, he was also trying to get published. And failing. In fact, he couldn't even get an agent.

"I would get a run of rejection letters and be depressed for ten days," he says, "then pull myself together and say, 'Okay, now what? I can quit. Or I can become a better writer, rewrite everything, send it to a new batch of agents, and see if I get in this time.'"

Each time he sent his fiction out to a new series of literary agents, he got a new round of rejections. Eventually, the rejection letters got better: from typewritten to handwritten, to phone calls, to meetings. Finally, he succeeded in signing with an agent. He showed the agent a novel he'd written, and the guy said, "I can give it a try, but you're an unknown writer; no publisher's going to be interested."

Kamal put his writing aside and, for the moment, forgot about it.

At this point, something interesting happened: One of those Silicon Valley companies he started did really well. *Really* well. And then the company blew up, taking all his money with it. The timing was terrible. He had just broken off a relationship. A close friend had recently died.

As you've probably guessed, this is where the "suck" part starts.

When Kamal's company fell apart, so did Kamal. He had been doing the classic entrepreneur thing for years, which is to say, working like a maniac without ever taking a break. Now the break took him. His health plummeted. The doctors he consulted could do nothing for him. He got worse. Some days he was so weak he could barely get around, and after only a few minutes outside he'd have to go back to bed.

Now, at the bottom of his pit, barely able to get out of bed, he decided to embrace the suck. Rather than try to climb out of the hole he'd dug himself into, rather than struggle to escape where he'd ended up, he made a radical decision: to put every one of the few ounces of energy he had left into *acceptance*. More than acceptance, in fact: love.

"I decided to love myself," he says. He spent the next few days, then weeks, pursuing a single-minded program of inner work focused on that singular idea: love yourself.

As he pulled out of his nosedive, the writer in him came back to life, and he wrote a short book about his process, which he titled *Love Yourself Like Your Life Depends On It*. He didn't even try to pitch this one to an agent; he simply published it himself on Amazon.

He had to work up the courage to push Publish. The idea of putting his little book out into the world was terrifying.

"Here I was, a complete failure, no money, I was going to have to go get a job, and I'm writing about the power of loving yourself? All my Silicon Valley peers would laugh me out of the room. It would destroy my career."

But he did it anyway.

Within a month, it was the No. 1 book in Amazon's Self-Help category. The book became a blockbuster bestseller.

"Those years of rejection letters were probably the best gift I ever got," says Kamal. It was that decade of writing and rewriting, striving to internalize Hemingway's economic, understated style, that taught him to write his story in such simple prose that it would appeal to a wide audience.

It wasn't just the suck of Kamal's epic collapse that he embraced. It was all those years of rejection slips, more than a decade of continuous feedback telling him he was failing; it was embracing *that* suck that gave him the tools he needed to create his ultimate success.

Since the book came out, Kamal has received thousands of e-mails from people telling him how reading it has changed their lives. "I got one from a seventy-two-year-old woman from the Isle of Man in the U.K., another from a sixteen-year-old girl in Ukraine," he says. The ones that really amaze him are the ones from older people, contacting him to say how after reading his book, they're having positive thoughts for the first time in their lives.

"I hear from a lot of men who've read my book, which in self-help is just unheard of. That surprised a lot of publishers," he adds, "but it doesn't surprise me."

With the success of *Love Yourself,* suddenly Kamal was in demand; rather than him chasing down an agent, now publishers were courting him. They wanted him to do another *Love Yourself* book, something else in the self-help field. He wouldn't do it. He had followed *Love Yourself* with the more meditative *Live Your Truth,* and that had been a fulfilling experience. But now he wanted to go beyond the self-help genre. He wanted to step it up, take it to the next level. To grow. So he took the better part of a year off to hole up and write a novel. *Rebirth: A Fable of Love, Forgiveness, and Following Your Heart* came out in January 2017. It's a hell of a read.

When I told Kamal we wanted to include this profile of him in a chapter called "Embrace the Suck," he said, "I've heard that phrase before. For me, though, it's not even the suck; it's just, your best moments are when you know you've given your all. Whether it's a product you built, or something like writing that you set out to do, or you're coaching your kid, whatever it is, you gave your all."

That's my cue. Kamal's comment about "coaching your kid" is where I leave his story and pick mine back up. Because of all the roles I've ever had, from search-and-rescue swimmer to SEAL platoon sniper to NSW sniper school course master to media CEO, none has been as important to me as the role of father.

From 2012 on, while I was working to build SOFREP and Hurricane Group from startup into a multimillion-dollar media business, I also pursued the path of rebuilding my relationship with my kids' amazing mother. Divorce sucks. You can try to run away from it. We have embraced it.

She has since remarried—a solid, terrific guy—and they now have the most beautiful little girl together. My daughter finally has a sister to help compete with her brothers. Our kids are doing incredibly well, and I spend more time with them than anyone ever imagined I would or could. They are strong and well-adjusted kids, healthy and happy, in large part because their mom and I get along and are aligned in our common goals around the family.

I'm so proud of them and the amazing people they are becoming.

Chapter 6
ONE TEAM, ONE FIGHT

The sound of the choppers slowly drains away, taking the last of the day's light and warmth with it. It is January 2002, and my SEAL platoon has been out in the mountains of Afghanistan since dawn with a twenty-man marine security team and a handful of techs, doing a one-day search-and-destroy sweep of the notorious al-Qaeda cave complex at Zhawar Kili. Those choppers were supposed to be for us, to take us back to base, but at the last minute command had them turn around and leave us out here to expand our mission. We only planned for a dawn-to-dusk operation. Now we're out here on our own for the night. (For over a week, as it will turn out.)

The commander who opted to accompany us at the last minute decides to take charge. "Okay," he says, "we'll go up into the hills and lay up in the bushes."

Our senior enlisted guy, Chief Dye, and I look at each other in disbelief. We are both thinking the same thing; I'm the one who opens his big mouth and says it.

"Hey, that's a bad idea. Our guys are freezing here, and it's going to get worse. If we just lay up in the bushes, we're going to have some cold casualties."

This commander, Smith, shakes his head. "We'll just have to suck it up."

Suck it up? This is a truly terrible idea. Nobody's brought any warm clothes or cold-weather gear, and temperatures have already dropped to near freezing. If we follow what this commander is saying, we're going to end up with some serious cases of hypothermia. But what are we supposed to do? There's a chain of command here. Strictly speaking, our No. 1 guy is our platoon OIC (officer in charge), Lieutenant Chris Cassidy. Then there's our assistant OIC, the No. 2 guy. Next comes Chief Dye. And me? I'm just one of the guys in the platoon. Commander Smith, even though he was not assigned to this mission and is not part of our platoon, has placed himself on top of that pyramid of command.

Chief Dye and I glance at each other again. This time he gives it a shot.

"Uh, sir, with all due respect, that idea sucks. Let me take Brandon and a few other guys, we'll go clear and occupy that village we saw today a few klicks away, and set up a perimeter so we have a place to light a fire and stay warm for the night."

"No," says Smith, "we're not going to do that—"

"*Yes we are.*" That's our OIC, Cassidy, giving the order. He doesn't give a shit if Smith outranks him. This is his platoon—and he's been listening to what his guys have to say. Cassidy nods at Chief Dye and me, and we set off to clear and secure the village, where we end up staying for the next week. And nobody freezes to death . . . not even Commander Smith.

Our week in Zhawar Kili turns out to be one of the most successful missions in the entire Afghanistan campaign. We capture or destroy roughly one million pounds of enemy ordnance and equipment, capture a ton of intelligence, and destroy one of the largest terrorist/military training facilities in the country. If our OIC hadn't listened to his team, it could have been cut off at the knees the first night out.

Unlike Smith, Cassidy is an excellent leader, one of the best I've had the honor of serving with. And unlike Smith, *he understands the value of his team.*

There's a popular image of the successful entrepreneur as a loner, a rugged individualist who bucks the trends of conventional thinking and goes it alone, ignoring the doubters and forging on to the beat of his own drum. The fool on the hill, as the Beatles put it. This goes really well with the American mythos of the lone frontiersman with his musket, beating back the savages and saving his farm against all odds.

Reality isn't like that.

We have a saying in the SEALs: "One team, one fight." This principle puts all the others in context, because no man or woman is an island, and no successful business is a solitary enterprise. It doesn't matter if you are in manufacturing or IT, marketing or service, technology or trucking: you are in the people business. No matter what your business model or your industry, people are key to your success. Having the right people is far more important than having the right tools, the right technology, the right plan, or the right financing. With the right people, you are unstoppable. With the wrong people, you are screwed. That naturally starts with hiring and working with the right people, but just as important as whom you work with is how you treat them.

In chapter 2, I mentioned Dale Carnegie's classic, *How to Win Friends and Influence People.* Sure, I know the book's been around forever, but there's a reason it's so popular: Carnegie nailed it. Success in business comes from caring about the other person and developing a legitimate, authentic relationship.

My friend Joe Apfelbaum, whom you met in chapter 1, says, "Don't look to build business; look to build relationships. The relationships will bring you the business. Learn to be great at *that.*" As usual, Joe is right on target.

I told you about the $15 million offer I had in the spring of 2014, but we didn't really get into why I turned it down.

When I was first contacted by an analyst for Scout Media, I couldn't work out exactly what the people at Scout were asking. It sounded as if they were talking about our partnering with them in some way. I wasn't interested, and said so. Soon after that, I got an e-mail from the CEO, who said the company was creating a big media roll-up targeted at men and they were interested in us as the military/outdoor component. They didn't want to do some vague joint venture. They wanted to acquire us.

The negotiations took a few weeks. The company flew me out to New York (I was still living and working in Nevada at the time) to see its operation and meet with its employees. I told them my number was $20 million. The CEO said, "What if I can give you fifteen, and a pathway to twenty?" I asked him for more details, and he put something together, mostly stock and some cash. We kept talking.

Something felt off.

For one, I didn't quite click with the CEO. Not that I didn't like the guy, but I had a sense that our core values didn't line up. It seemed to me that these people were purely financially driven. Don't get me wrong: I like making money. I like it a lot. But it's not my No. 1 driving force.

Here are the four core values we subscribe to at Hurricane:

People First. *We take care of our audience, sponsors, partners, friends, and family. This gives us a strong foundation in all we do.*

Honesty and Integrity. *Both are valued in everything we do, and we see doing the right thing and brutal honesty as competitive advantages.*

No Limits. *We see endless possibilities to what we can create together. We are solution-based thinkers, welcoming new ideas and personal growth.*

Giving Back. *We are committed to giving back to military and civic charitable causes that align with our core values. We want to help make America a better place to live.*

Financial profit *is* important; do you see it in here? It's in value No. 3, "No Limits: We see endless possibilities to what we can create together." That includes creating top-dollar financial return. But there's a reason that value is No. 3 and "People First" comes first on this list: it's because *it comes first*.

This shows, for example, in how we relate to our customer base.

We have a highly engaged audience, which is exactly how I like it. This morning when I stepped out for coffee, I ran into a SOFREP fan at the coffee shop. Here was this dude, dressed in a business suit, meeting with other businesspeople—and he interrupted their meeting to come over and say hello. "Hey, you're Brandon Webb, right?" he said. "I read your book, and listen, I love what you guys are doing at SOFREP."

I *love* that.

And I worried about that. I wanted to take care of this community we'd built. I had a relationship with my audience and my customers, and I was concerned about whether Scout would take care of them or just treat them as a number.

Then there was my staff. I'd put a lot into building this group, and I cared about them like brothers. How would this deal affect them? Would I be putting them in a situation where they had to work for someone who wasn't a good fit?

Instinctively, I already knew the answer.

I declined the offer.

You know what happened next. Scout raised some money, part of which came from a group of Russian investors who turned around and fired the CEO, threw the executive team out, and started from scratch on their own terms. If I'd gone down that road, all our hard work at Hurricane would have wound up in the dustbin of entrepreneurial history. (To appropriate a phrase from an old Russian takeover artist.)

It's now more than two years later, and our business is thriving—and so are our staff and our community.

Treat Your People Like Family

Executives pay major bucks to learn from consultants who promise to tell them the secrets to creating a strong company culture. Everyone knows that culture is a company's lifeblood, and everyone wants to know the inside story, the tricks of the trade, the secret sauce. How did Apple do it? How did Zappos do it? How did Southwest do it?

But you don't need to spend a hundred grand to get this. It's pretty simple. We have a pretty low turnover rate at my company. The people on our team who have stuck, who've been around for years now, are tremendously devoted to the company. People ask me why. Here's why: I treat them like family.

One of our people recently went through a really bad divorce. "Look," I told him, "don't worry. I've got your back." I gave him some stock options to help nail down his situation, just so he wouldn't feel as if he were going off a cliff. This wasn't promised or even expected. I just did it. At the same time, I gave some stock options to another team member who had been working with us for a while and had gone way above and beyond the call of duty. I told them both, "You guys are getting this because you've earned it, and I want to take care of you."

One of my IT people in the Philippines had to have a minor procedure. It was only $300, but for him that was a lot of money. I told him not to worry about it. If this was my brother, or my son, what would I do? I'd take care of it. Case closed.

These guys treat the business as if it were their own. It *is* their own. They treat it the way I treat them.

Hurricane Group is a digital business, which allows us to operate with our team physically spread out all over the planet. Ben, our COO, is in Connecticut. Jason, our brand director, is in Oregon. Drew, our SOFREP-TV director, is in Boston. Our media director Nick is in Lake Tahoe. Emily, our customer service person, lives in Indiana. My personal assistant Angie is in Pennsylvania. We have sales guys in Massachusetts and Arizona. We have writers all over the world, from Iraq to Japan. All our tech is in the Philippines.

Which is great, because it gives people a lot of freedom—but it also could be a handicap if I let it, because nothing can really replace the experience of being face-to-face in a room together.

So we address that. When we hire someone new, he or she meets with me and the core team, in person, right away. Unless you've sat down with people, talked with them about their kids, their spouse or girlfriend, their life, and humanized that experience, then they don't tend to work as closely together. It's hard to let someone down if you've had that person-to-person interaction, even if you then go work on your own.

In the SEAL teams, it didn't matter if you were a sniper or a heavy weapons gunner, if you were part of the team, you were part of the team. We all trained hard together, fought hard together, and had hard fun together. That built chemistry and alignment, and it created an unbreakable bond within the SEAL platoon environment. I've sought to create the same in my business with team-building events, dinners, outings, and creative off-site meetings. (Skydiving, anyone?)

Once a year, we have a strategy meeting, and everyone who's core comes to that. We do a two-day retreat—this year it was at my home in Puerto Rico—where we have a series of structured meetings and then all go out and have a great dinner together. Every year I throw a holiday party for everybody. This year I'm flying in all the spouses and significant others.

We do a lot of videoconferencing, which helps. One guy who's been with me for four years, Cris, I flew over here from the Philippines so we could spend some time together. It was his first time in America and he had an absolute blast, did the whole tourist thing in spades, posting photos on social media of every location you can imagine. But even before we did this, things were already solid: we'd developed a close connection just through phone and Skype. It took a little more effort to establish, because we'd never been in the same room together—hell, we'd never been in the same *country* together— but we did it.

Take Hiring Seriously

My experience in the military taught me that people are not what they say or what they put on their résumé. They are what they do. And not just what they do right now, today, sitting across from me in a coffee shop booth or at a boardroom table as we conduct our interview, but three weeks from now, three months from now, when they're on the phone with a customer or a client.

In other words, you have to base your hiring decision on behavior you won't get to witness until well after the decision is made. It's a conundrum. What do you do?

You take the interview seriously.

When I finally earned my Navy SEAL Trident, after making it through BUD/S and then six more months of intense post-BUD/S training, I had to go before a board of crusty, grizzled Vietnam-era SEALs. These guys ate cigarettes for breakfast after running fifteen miles in the soft sand. When it was my turn to go before the review board, they asked me some of the toughest scenario-based questions I've ever been asked. They grilled me hard.

"What would you do if you saw a fellow teammate take drugs?"

"If you had total failure in your closed-circuit [bubbleless] breathing device and had to surface in an enemy harbor, how would you handle the situation without compromising your fellow teammates?"

"What would you do if a superior officer asked you to take out a civilian who wasn't an immediate threat?"

The hard questions kept coming. What they were doing was brilliant: while they were deciding whether or not they wanted to work with me, they were also painting a portrait of the kind of SEAL I would be. It was an incredible experience, and I use a similar format when I interview a prospective hire whom I haven't had the chance to work with in the past. I ask questions that force critical thinking, induce stress (a favorite technique from my sniper instructor days), and allow the interviewer to slowly build background on what the person is really like. I want to get as much insight as I can into who he really is. Is he passionate about what he does? What kind of standard does he hold for himself? How does he think?

For example, here's a question for a prospective digital advertising sales executive: "What would you do if the decision maker on your biggest account asked you to lie for him?"

One of my favorite interview questions (which I got from an Australian entrepreneur friend) is, "Do you believe in aliens?" I love it, because you can't get around with an easy yes or no; it forces a thoughtful reply, and that's what I want to see. (You'd be amazed at the answers and rationales I've heard!) I don't really care whether the prospective employees believe in aliens or not, but it opens up a fascinating window into what kinds of people they are, how creative they are, what kinds of minds they have.

When Betsy Morgan was in the process of leaving CBS and looking for what to do next, she spent months going through a lengthy recruiting process at Apple, where she was interviewing for the position of running iTunes. This was 2007, the year the first iPhone shipped, and there was a lot of buzz about what Apple was up to. Every month or so, Betsy would get another call saying, "Hey, can you come out and meet so-and-so?"

Finally, after nine months of this, she got a call asking if she could come out for one last interview. The caller said, "We want you to come meet with Steve."

So she flew out to Apple headquarters in Cupertino and spent an hour talking with Steve Jobs.

He didn't ask her a thing about her work at CBS, or her work anywhere, for that matter. He said, "Listen, if you're going to be a top executive in this company, I want to know who you are. I want to know what keeps you up at night. I want to know what your values are. I want to know what you care about." They talked about things like: When did you first fall in love? What cities have you visited? For an hour they talked about . . . well, about everything. About their lives.

At the end of the summer, she was offered the job, but by then her mom had fallen critically ill, and she realized that she just couldn't leave the East Coast for a job in California. It was a heart-wrenching decision, but she had to decline the position.

She says she'll remember that conversation for the rest of her life. That's the kind of impression I want prospective employees to take away from an interview: this isn't just a verbal punch list of skill sets and qualifications—it's a probing conversation to learn as much as possible about who this person *is*.

Hire People Who Fit Your Culture

When I was a freshly minted SEAL, stationed at SEAL Team Three in Coronado, I saw an entire sixteen-man SEAL platoon disbanded because it just wasn't working. This is *SEALs*, remember, men who have already gone through one of the most rigorous and demanding selection processes in the world. There was no mediocrity here. It was just that there were people in the unit who weren't meshing. The chemistry wasn't there.

In a way, the men on this SEAL team were extremely fortunate: leadership had the option to disband and restructure this team before its weak chemistry did any lasting harm. In business, it often doesn't work that way, and dysfunctional teams like this all too often inflict mortal damage on the company. Which is why it is so important to hire people who fit your culture in the first place.

It's crucial to have chemistry in any organization. In SEAL teams, lives are on the line. In a business, the life of that business is just as much on the line. Creating a business that survives and thrives is only going to happen when you have employees who genuinely enjoy doing their work, and that is only going to happen when the chemistry works.

I talked in chapter 4 about hiring only excellent people, people who will do a stellar job and raise the level of the company, not lower it. But it's not just about excellence. It's also about finding people who are coachable and who are a solid fit with the company culture. Typically, a company's culture starts with the founder, but it can't end there. Ultimately, the culture has to be carried by the people who work at the company. Your culture may be defined by your stated core values—but only if those core values actually express themselves through what your people do and how they behave day in and day out. Values don't do any good sitting on the page.

I recently hired an extremely smart and productive employee. Within two months, I fired him, based purely on his poor treatment of another employee, a trusted team member who had been with me for years. This guy was talented (and knew it), but he didn't know how to respect other people and work as part of a team. I saw the early warning signs and took swift action to resolve the situation. Yes, we lost a talent, but talent is easy to replace. Esprit de corps and a solid team ethos are too precious to let anything threaten them. A team with average ability but great chemistry will win out over a team with extreme talent but lousy chemistry. Character counts more than talent, and attitude counts more than skill.

Another example: I interviewed someone to work remote ad sales. She showed up at our interview a little bit late and disheveled looking. To me this was a red flag, and my gut said no, but she'd come strongly recommended from my sales guy, who said she could really sell, so I overrode my gut, went with the recommendation, and put her on a sixty-day trial on retainer.

Turned out, my sales guy and my gut were both right. She really *could* sell, but I started getting customer complaints that she was too abrasive. I told her, "Look, I'm sorry but this isn't working out." She sued me (using age discrimination as the basis), but it never got to court. Remember when I said sometimes it makes more sense to settle than fight? This was one of those times. I settled and moved on. Worth it.

This taught me a lesson: to make sure we *always* choose people who mesh with our existing culture. That is a lesson we have followed to the letter ever since.

We recently hired a customer service ambassador, Emily. This position was so important that we interviewed ten people for it, and there were some great people in the mix. But Emily was clearly the best fit. She was a military spouse, which was a plus, but more than that, it was evident that she really cared about our customer base. That authentic caring is something you can't fake. People try all the time, with slogans and lifetime guarantees and canned scripts, but you can't build that kind of attitude with corporate Legos and Tinkertoys. It has to be real, from the person him- or herself.

It's really pretty simple: if you're genuinely willing to go the extra mile, people notice that and appreciate it.

To me, the true litmus test of a company's culture is the "hit by a bus" scenario: If the founder were hit by a bus tomorrow, would your company culture continue without you, or would the mice come out and play? Steve Jobs's passing is an excellent example; the culture he created at Apple continues today. Sure, Tim Cook and whoever succeeds Tim will have to continue fostering it, but I'm betting that what Jobs built culturally will survive for decades to come. Everyone knows what Apple stands for as a brand, consumers and employees alike. Part of that is the strength and total focus of Jobs's personality—but a bigger part of it is that he successfully built up a company of people who bought into his vision wholeheartedly.

Don't Wait Long to Fire Someone Who Isn't Working Out

There's been a lot of buzz, both positive and negative, around the phrase "hire slow, fire fast," and as with most catchphrases there's both truth and bullshit to it. Sometimes you can't afford the luxury of hiring slow, because you need the position filled *now*. I wouldn't necessarily recommend hiring slow; I say, hire carefully. Hire with thoroughness and patience. Even if you have to do it damn fast, like tomorrow, you can still be careful and thorough.

But fire fast? Yeah, I definitely go with that one.

One of the biggest mistakes you can make in business is to wait too long to fire someone who isn't working out. In my experience, a problem employee spreading hate and discontent is cancer to the organism, and the quicker you get rid of that employee, the better off your business is, and the better off the employee is, too. (Don't kid yourself: you're doing the other person no favor by prolonging the inevitable.) One bad apple can demoralize the entire team and bring down the performance of your operation. When there's a problem, I deal with it, completely and immediately. *Violence of action.*

Early in Fighter Sweep's history, our editor got a big head. We had a lot of active-duty guys writing for him, and the site grew to the point where we were able to put him on a part-time retainer. Which was a great step, but we obviously wanted it to go further. The plan was to grow the site to the point where it had enough traffic to support itself, then use that demonstrable traffic to land an anchor sponsor, and then bring him on full-time.

We had just about gotten to that point when I got a call from our managing editor, Desiree. "Hey, Brandon, I'm concerned about this guy."

She said this editor was bitching about my flying around in my plane, as if I were some kind of billionaire showing off. (For the record: I'd worked hard for the money to buy that little plane, which I purchased for cash; I didn't even own a car; and at the time I was taking less than minimum wage in salary from the business.) He was harboring all this resentment about me, smiling to my face, and then trash-talking me behind my back—to my own team!

I asked my COO, Ben, to talk to him. Ben gave it a shot, then came back and said, "This guy's not salvageable."

I had Desiree talk to him one more time and explain to the guy that we were just about to make him a full-time offer. His reply was, "I'll only come on if Brandon is prepared to meet my demands."

Meet my demands?

I called him up and fired him that same day.

He was on location for some big aviation event where he was being treated like a VIP. I got him on the phone and said, "Look, you're done, and here are the reasons why. I'm sorry, man, but that's how it is."

I don't think he was expecting that.

People tend to overestimate their own worth to an enterprise. (I saw this quite a bit when I worked in the defense industry.) The best place to be, when you're part of an organization, is to be irreplaceable. He might have thought he was in that category, but he wasn't. I had him replaced in ten minutes.

Become an Excellent Judge of Character

To achieve what you're here to do, you need to become an excellent judge of character. If you don't already have this ability, you'll develop it. You'll *have* to. Learn to listen to your gut instinct—but don't necessarily trust your first impression. People can surprise you.

I've gotten much better at evaluating people quickly, whether or not they're a good fit. How do you do this? Same way you do anything. Practice. With everyone you interact with, do business with, ask yourself, *Who is this person? What are her values? What's important to her? How does she interact with other people?* The more you ask those questions, the better you'll get at knowing the answers.

One of the best lessons I learned in the military was *never* judge a person by his appearance. If you lined up the two hundred plus starting students in my BUD/S class, chances are excellent that you'd never have picked out the twenty plus who made it all the way through training and became Navy SEALs. Me included. You never know what people are capable of until they show you, or until they demonstrate it through some other credible means, such as school grades and verifiable work achievements. Frankly, I place a much higher value on the "until they show you" side. Past accomplishments and credentials are a solid way to judge if someone is worthy of your trust, but don't go in blindly.

So many people told me I would never make it through the qualifications and become a Navy SEAL. Many more told me I would fail at business. You know what most of those naysayers said when I eventually became successful? "I always knew you'd make it."

(Uh-huh. Sure you did.) You'll run into these doubters yourself. Use their negative comments like kindling to stoke your internal fire and help you succeed at whatever you set out to accomplish.

To "never judge on appearances," I would add another important caveat: never judge someone based on rumors. I've seen so many good people taken down by vicious (and false) stories, viral bits of pseudo-information fueled by nothing but jealousy and personal self-worth issues on the part of the rumormonger. I have been a target of this destructive process myself and know firsthand just how nasty people can get. Sometimes those rumors follow people from one workplace to the next, through no fault of their own. Don't buy it. Investigate, and form your own opinion.

You'd think this would be an easy one for people to figure out, but surprisingly it's not. Human beings are a social species. We love to talk, and it's part of human nature to spread the news, both the good and the bad. Especially the juicy stuff. It may be a natural impulse, but it's one that a good leader works diligently to eradicate. Spreading rumors and gossip without verifying the source and motive is foolish. You are whom you hang out with; avoid the bottom-feeders.

You also have to develop the judgment to know where each person fits in the organization and what he wants to do. This was something I've had to learn by doing—that is, by realizing I was doing it wrong. I've looked at people I was hiring and said, "This person is really talented; he can do anything," which might well have been true, but just because someone *can* fulfill a certain role doesn't mean that's going to be fulfilling *for him*.

For a while, I had Jack, our editor in chief, doing a lot of management tasks—things that a managing editor would typically take care of. It didn't take long to realize he was miserable in this role. Jack is a brilliant writer and majorly talented in a dozen directions. But having him doing the kinds of things a managing editor does— measuring output every day, tracking which author has done how many posts, keeping track of our freelance budget—was driving him crazy. On the other hand, Desiree, our managing editor, is great at that stuff and has a natural feel for it. I don't think I've ever seen Jack as happy as he was the day she came on board. I was, too, because if Jack had had to stay in that role much longer, I don't know if I would have been able to keep him.

I see a lot of people put in roles that, yeah, they *can* do, but they're not really excited about. That's a big mistake; long term, it never works out. Just because you think someone will be great at something doesn't mean he wants to do it.

Reward People the Way *They* Want, Not the Way *You* Want

The way I've set up our business gives our employees a lot of autonomy, and to some people that's very appealing. That's another reason we have such a low turnover rate.

I met our brand director, Jason, when he was freelancing for a client of ours. I saw how good his work was. He was having some turmoil in his life and needed flexibility in his schedule that the client couldn't give him—but I could. I hired him away. Since then, I've hired away two more guys from that same firm. There are good people out there, and if you create an environment where they'll be happier to work than where they are now, they'll join you. Especially if you support their extracurricular passions.

It's not a question of offering more money. Compensation is important, but good money isn't everything. Take Jason: I told him he was so valuable to us that I was giving him a raise at the end of the year. "Look," he said, "I really appreciate that, but I also have to tell you, for me a lot of it is that I get the chance here to create and execute a lot of cool ideas." He's a creative type, and the artistic fulfillment of the job matters a lot to him.

For Nick, our media director, the "compensation" that matters most is the freedom to be able to take time off and go do things on his own. For example, I know he wants to go to Burning Man every year. I also know that when he comes back, it takes a while to get himself back into gear, and every year I have to crack the whip on him for a few days. He knows it, I know it, and we laugh about it— and I let him go back every year. It's worth it.

I don't give out big cash bonuses at the end of the year. Instead, we have a nice dinner together, and I buy people personal gifts—not just the standard sort of bullshit generic gift, but something I've given a lot of thought to picking out for each person, a gift that means something to that person. Something he's interested in, something heartfelt that he'll remember. And, typically, expensive. I've bought quite a few watches for people. It's something they genuinely appreciate—and because it's on their wrists every day they always remember where it came from. (At Hurricane, a watch from Brandon has come to signify "You're officially on the team.")

Another key piece of compensation, if you want to call it that, is praise: genuine praise, well deserved, not just gratuitous glad-handing. We have a meeting with our core team every Monday, and every Monday I make the effort to find something that someone's done that I can publicly recognize. I go out of my way to let people know I appreciate their hard work, or their loyalty, or their ingenuity in solving a tough problem, or whatever it is that I notice. (And by the way, everyone on the core team also meets with *his* team weekly and duplicates this process.) It's so easy just to file away the observation and say nothing in the moment, because you're busy, and you figure, hey, you'll wait for the right time. But you're always busy. The "right time" never comes. I've gotten into the habit of putting the thought in an e-mail right away. "Hey, thanks for doing that; as always you have my back and I see that and appreciate it."

It goes a long way. People want to be appreciated.

Choose Business Partners as Carefully as a Marriage Partner

Sometimes I ask myself, if I were starting the Wind Zero project today, from scratch, with what I know now, what would I do differently? The answer is easy. I would vet potential partners *very* carefully, and I would end up with different partners from the ones I actually worked with.

In my ten years of post-military business life, I've had partners who actively sabotaged me (at Wind Zero); an early writing partner who was so problematic I had to break a publishing contract to sever my ties with him; a friend who participated in some early SOFREP TV videos and then sued me for them; an old BUD/S teammate who mounted a vicious smear campaign against me (not the Wind Zero one, another one since then); and a core player from my original SOFREP team whom I eventually had to let go.

All of these were painful experiences, but they were also a critically important education. One of the most important decisions you'll ever make in your business is your choice of partners. On the field of battle, the wrong partner will get you killed. In business, the wrong partner will sink you. I've picked the wrong partner. And I've picked the right partner. One decision nearly ruined me. The other has taken my business to a whole new level.

I see so many people in business getting involved in instant partnerships. They meet someone at a networking event and get talking about an idea, and next thing you know, they're in a venture together. I'm watching this from the sidelines and thinking, *Oh, boy, I see where this is going.* Because I've been down that road.

The other day I was talking with an entrepreneur who's starting a new project, and he said, "Hey, I'm looking for a partner on this, if you know somebody, let me know."

I said, "So you're just throwing this out there, like you're willing to jump into bed with anyone who comes along? Man, that's a recipe for disaster."

I'll make this simple: think of a partnership as a marriage. This isn't like hiring an employee. You're going into this thing together till death do you part. I'm no expert on marriage, but I do know this: you don't marry someone after two or three dates. You can't know if a given relationship is going to be worthwhile, dependable, in alignment, and valuable enough to raise it to the status of a genuine partnership until you've spent some serious time together.

As the old knight told Indy, "Choose wisely."

Treat Your Customers Like Family, Too

There is no separate chapter in this book on how to treat your customers, because this *is* that chapter. And it's not "A few teams, one fight." It's *one* team, one fight. Your customers are *part* of your team, just like your employees, contractors, partners, suppliers, and shareholders.

When we started our gear club, we went through a period when our fulfillment wasn't well sorted out yet. E-mail got out of control, our customer service couldn't keep up, and hundreds of e-mails were going unanswered. People were messaging us on Facebook, saying they couldn't get hold of us through our regular system. It was bad. It wasn't that we didn't care; the thing just grew way faster than expected, and we got swamped.

I started taking the really nasty complaints myself. My approach was simple: I would flat-out own it and then offer to do whatever it would take to satisfy the customer, even if it meant losing him. "Look, we fucked up," I'd say. "What can we do to make it up to you?" In most cases, the customers were shocked that it was me calling them or e-mailing them. Why was the CEO reaching out to them? But there isn't any function more important than customer service.

We dealt with it aggressively, threw ourselves at it full force (that was when we hired Emily), and before long reversed the tide.

Still, service is never perfect; there are always glitches. And I've stayed involved. In the past month, I've had probably ten customer interactions with people who got pissed off about one thing or another: they got their box late, or they signed up for a digital subscription and no one got back to them so they couldn't log in. I approach it the same way, every time: I own it. "We let you down. What can we do to make it up to you?"

Ten times out of ten, it saved that customer, because he could tell I was genuine about it. Whatever we can do to make it up. One guy said in his e-mail that he was "ready to punch somebody." I wrote back and said, "Hey, before you punch anyone, let's get this sorted out." He LOL'ed back, and we got it sorted out. "I can't believe you are taking the time to write me," he said. Of course I am. It's important.

Another reason you have to communicate with your customers is that it's the only way you'll know what they really want. Too often businesses assume they know what the customer wants, usually because it's what *they* would want. But you are not your customer.

I went out the other day to buy some ski boots. While I was waiting to get fitted, I stepped over to the coffee shop next door and ordered a small mocha. The guy screwed up my order, apologized, and made it over again, only this time he handed over a giant mocha in this huge cup. "Hey, I gave you the extra-large size," he said, as if he'd done something wonderful.

But I didn't want a giant mocha; I wanted a small. That's what I ordered. A large was too many calories. Now I had to carry this awkward, big-ass coffee around, and it wasn't the one I wanted.

The point is, he thought he was doing me this big favor. He didn't understand what I really wanted, because he didn't take the time to ask. He thought he was giving great service. He wasn't. He was actually giving me lousy service; he just didn't know it.

Put Trust and Loyalty in Front of Everything Else

In the military, it didn't take more than a moment to establish trust with others, because the people I worked with wore their accomplishments right on their uniforms in the form of award ribbons and rank insignias. That made it a hell of a lot easier to trust someone right off the bat.

It doesn't work that way in the civilian world. Trust has to be established by some other measure, and like the SEAL pin I used to wear, you have to keep earning that trust every day.

Some people simply don't get this. A good leader never forgets it.

Trust is an incredibly valuable gift and should be cherished as such. You need to earn the trust others place in you every day. In business, I see so many people who view trust as something they can simply bank on once it's been established, as if they can slack off from that point on and don't need to continue demonstrating that they are trustworthy. Learn to spot these people quickly, and stay away from them. They are not who you want on your team or in your life.

Trust goes hand in hand with loyalty. I'm surprised how readily some people change teams and say, "Hey, it's not personal; it's business." Let me offer some perspective: That's a bullshit statement. It's *all* personal. Business is made of people; there is no such thing as business that isn't personal.

This is a key I've observed in those who are tremendously successful in business: they establish a small group of extremely loyal and trustworthy friends (sometimes in the same industry, but more often not), and they value that small circle over those who are in only until the chips are down. This isn't just true for business; it's true for anything you do.

I once gave a talk about teamwork and leadership to some players and coaches in the Nike high school basketball program. These were the best coaches and teams in America. After my talk, the Nike representative told me that in previous years a few of his sponsored teams had switched to different sponsors, only to realize how much value they had given up in leaving Nike. And when they came back, hat in hand? He said he was sorry but could no longer offer them a sponsorship. They had broken loyalty. To Nike, this is a core value and an extremely important one. Nike is smart, and that's part of why it has such a powerful brand.

I've sought to apply what that rep told me to my own core values. I've had more than a few people, some of whom I placed a lot of trust in, try to get back into my inner circle after a break in loyalty, and I've compassionately turned each of them away. Hold true to your own core values and make no exceptions. People will respect you more for it.

I've told you about that terrible day when my wife and I took our kids to a park they didn't know and told them that our marriage was over. As I said, it was one of the worst days of my life. But our family didn't end that day. After we said what we were there to say, and they cried, and we did, too, in the end we all hugged together as a family, and that was the moment when the healing began. We made a commitment to the kids right then and there that no matter what happened, we were still a family. And they believed us. It hurt like hell, but it got a little better each day from that moment on—because we made sure they knew that we were both still there for them, and they trusted that we meant it.

PROFILE: RYAN ZAGATA (BROOKLYN BICYCLE COMPANY)

When I joined EO New York in December 2014, Ryan Zagata was one of the first people I got to know. I met him at the group's holiday party, and we hit it off instantly.

Ryan was a high-performing software sales guy, living in Manhattan, when he and his wife, Thea, faced the fact that raising a family in Manhattan just wasn't going to make economic sense. For the kind of home they wanted, they were going to have to relocate over the East River to Brooklyn. Ryan loved the energy and vibrancy of life in Manhattan and says he left kicking and screaming.

But then something interesting happened. Within a week of moving to Brooklyn, he had fallen in love. Brooklyn had all the energy, the culture, the restaurants, everything he'd loved about Manhattan, but it also had a small-city, close-knit-community feel that reminded him of the neighborhoods of Syracuse, in upstate New York, where he grew up.

He spent his first few months there walking an eighteen-block radius around his home, getting the feel for his new neighborhood, checking out every nook and cranny. When he wanted to extend that reach, he bought a bike, which enabled him to expand his explorations to a thirty-block and then forty-block radius.

"That bicycle became a way to meet new people," he says, "to find new restaurants, scout out new parks where we would take our children as our family grew—to get around, see things, experience things, connect with more people and more neighborhoods."

This was 2008. Over the next few years, as the country plunged into recession, Ryan found himself enjoying his software business less and less. When Thea, a publicist by profession, started her own baking business, Ryan was intrigued. He'd always had an engineering bent; when he was a kid, he loved to take things apart and see how they worked. In college, that morphed into an interest in business; he would read copies of business magazines cover to cover, seeing if he could take companies apart to see what made them work or, if they were not successful, what made them fail to work. Now that interest surfaced again. Soon Thea told him, "Ryan, you're way more interested in this business than I am. You need to start your own company!"

Ryan liked the idea. The question was, his own business doing what?

In January 2011, he and Thea took a little time off to do some traveling overseas. While in Vietnam, he saw people getting around on simple, no-frills bikes, and he commented to Thea, "See, *that's* the bike I really wanted. No bells and whistles, just something simple and serviceable—not for racing, not for cross-country biking, just for getting around town and seeing neighborhoods."

A month later, back in the States, he incorporated his bicycle business, and it took off like a shot.

His first year, asked by his insurance agent to make a sales projection for insurance purposes, he said, "I don't know. Seventy-five thousand dollars?" It seemed an enormous goal. They finished out the year at over $200,000 and have been growing ever since. Brooklyn Bicycle Company has become a very cool brand, with its products showcased as fashion accessories in *Vogue* (in a 2012 issue, Ryan's "Willow blue" bike was touted as the ideal match for a Thakoon Panichgul dress; go figure), written up in the *New York Times*, featured in the Museum of Modern Art, and spotted with various New York celebrities astride them.

But what's interesting to me—and the reason I picked Ryan to write about in this chapter—is how his core values have shaped the evolution of the company.

At first, his plan was to sell bikes online, direct to consumer. But bicycles are not like furniture, where it's no big deal if the consumer messes it up a little. If you don't assemble a bicycle properly, there can be serious consequences. There were already plenty of companies selling bikes online for customer assembly, and Ryan saw bikes on the street that had been put together with the front wheel on backward so the fork was pointing the wrong way. It made him cringe. "You don't want someone rolling out into traffic on a bike that hasn't been put together correctly," he says.

So rather than the direct-to-consumer model, he focused on building a network of dealers. When you bought a Brooklyn bike, Ryan would look for the nearest dealer to you, ship it there, and pay that shop to assemble it for you, to make sure you got a good experience. Which meant that Brooklyn Bicycle Company began developing a whole web of relationships—partnerships, really—with bicycle dealers all over the region, and soon all over the country. Beyond simply selling bicycles, Ryan's business became a vehicle to help all these dealers build *their* businesses.

At the same time, he found that what he loved most about his company was watching the people he hired grow in their roles, professionally and personally as well as financially. He tended to hire people who were young, one or two years out of college—very green, very hungry, and very eager.

"I couldn't throw lavish amounts of money or big chunks of equity at someone," he says, "or feed them the story that we were going to be the next Bloomberg. What I told them was that they would have the opportunity to *grow* here—to be involved in the decision-making process and play a broad role in the direction of the company, not just come in and do a job."

For example, he hired a young woman named Emily Rose to work in operations. She was passionate, enthusiastic, and crackerjack smart. Ryan was looking around to hire an experienced marketing person. Instead, one day he turned to Emily and said, "Hey, are you interested in marketing?" She was. "Cool," said Ryan. "You are now doing marketing. Let's get you some courses so you can learn more about it. We'll figure it out together."

Ryan didn't know much more about marketing than she did, but he encouraged her to find a mentor, a director of marketing at a bigger company they admired, and she took some courses, too. She has flourished in that role, and Ryan says it was one of the best business decisions he's ever made.

Ryan's company plowed along for more than two years without having a clearly defined mission. Not that he hadn't tried to pin one down. He knew as well as anyone that every business needs a compelling mission, and he'd tried many times to articulate one, but each attempt fizzled. He came up with statements that looked good on paper but just didn't resonate.

One day an entrepreneur friend started quizzing him as to what had led him to start the company. What made him want a bicycle in the first place? Suddenly it clicked—and Ryan had his company's mission. Just six words: "We connect people with their neighborhoods."

Those six words transformed his business. Suddenly aspects of the operation that he had wrestled with for months sorted themselves out, guided by the clarity that statement provided. Lingering brand ambiguities cleared up, new approaches to marketing suggested themselves, and he saw new strategies for how to engage with his company's dealers.

"I realized that our company wasn't about bicycles," he says. "It was about helping people build relationships with the other people around them—their neighborhoods."

Of course, you could drive around. But in a car, as Ryan points out, you tend to hop in and flip on the radio, and before you know it, you've arrived at your destination, without a thought to anything you passed by in the process. You could also walk, as he did in his first few months in Brooklyn. But walking limits your reach. Riding a bike provides the ability to interact (like walking) as well as extend and vary your routes (like a car), which adds up to a unique experience you can't get any other way. It lets you connect with your neighborhood.

Ryan did not come from a family of businesspeople; his father was a public school teacher and basketball coach, and his mother, a pediatric nurse. I mention that I detect the DNA of both in his business model: the coach shows up in how he builds up and roots for everyone on his team—employees, dealers, and customers—and there's that nurse's genuine sense of nurturing underlying everything he does.

"I guess that's true," he says. "The world has become very transactional: you click a few buttons; the next day a T-shirt shows up at your door." Ryan says one of his goals at Brooklyn Bicycle Company is to create more experiences that are transformational and not simply transactional.

"When someone calls our office," he adds, "there's no chance they'll go to another brand. They will never buy another bicycle from anyone else, because of the experience they had with us. And that's not 'brand loyalty'; it's the sense they get that we genuinely care about them, that someone's got their back. That if something goes wrong, we'll be there to pick them up—and whenever something goes right, we'll be there to high-five them."

Chapter 7

LEAD FROM THE FRONT

✤ ● ✤

Twenty fourteen was a terrible year, and I didn't see it coming. Hell, I didn't see it while it was happening.

Our first year with SOFREP had been phenomenal. When I launched the site in February 2012, I had the feeling it would find a solid following, but it caught on even beyond my expectations. Growth was explosive. By the end of the year, we had put up about a thousand posts and were getting about two million page views and 300,000 unique visitors per month. Total revenue for the year was well over half a million dollars.

The growth continued into the following year. By the end of 2013, our single site had blossomed into multiple sites under the new Hurricane Group umbrella, SOFREP Radio and our digital publishing arm were both going strong, and our risky move to a paid-subscription model had gone extremely well. Business was booming on every front, and I fully expected the growth to keep on going.

It didn't.

In terms of both exposure and revenue, 2014 should have been an up year. Instead, growth flatlined. By three months into the year, I should have seen what was happening. One consistently terrible quarter should have set all my alarm bells ringing. Instead, I let things go for the whole year, until it was almost too late.

The truth was, I was in a slump. A big part of that was personal. As I said earlier, Glen's death in Benghazi in the fall of 2012 changed my life—but it took me a few years to realize just how much it had affected me. At the time it happened, it was obvious how consuming the whole thing was: breaking the news to some of our close mutual friends and to my kids (who loved him like family) . . . being part of the memorial services . . . writing an open letter to Glen that was published in the *New York Times* . . . becoming involved in helping his family through those times with my Red Circle Foundation . . . writing about Benghazi and seeing the whole event get hijacked by political hacks during an election season . . . on and on and on. Losing my girlfriend, Nadine, an incredibly talented and beautiful woman whom I unwittingly pushed away. There were a thousand things that fall that revolved around Glen's death and its aftermath.

But then 2012 turned to 2013; the news cycle continued churning along as the seasons turned. Life went on. And so did I—or at least I thought so. Until the end of 2014, when the year-end reports from Hurricane hit me like a cold shower, and I realized that I had been out of it, in more ways than one.

I knew I was still hurting over Glen's death. What I hadn't seen was how much that had been affecting me—not only emotionally, but also in my performance. I had let myself get mired down in the details of the business. I wasn't paying enough attention to the big picture. I wasn't leading the business; I was being sucked along in its wake.

Maybe you've heard the joke about the guy who went golfing with his friend Fred. He gets home after a long Saturday looking worn and haggard. His wife asks him how his day on the links was.

"Terrible," he says. "Things were going fine until we got to the seventh hole, when Fred keeled over. Coronary. He was dead by the time he hit the ground."

"Oh my God!" his wife exclaims. "That *is* terrible!"

"Yeah," says her husband. "From that point on, it was hit the ball and drag Fred, hit the ball and drag Fred, hit the ball and drag Fred . . ."

That's what was happening throughout 2014. SOFREP was hitting the ball and dragging Brandon. I needed to get back out in front of the curve, to start driving momentum again, the way I had in year one. I needed to do what all good leaders do.

I needed to lead from the front.

You Have to Earn Your Title Every Day

Of all the SEAL slogans that have been popularized over the last few years, probably the most famous is "The only easy day was yesterday." That one has its counterpart in business: "You're only as good as your last deal." Only I would change that slightly, because the reality is, you're only as good as your *next* deal. You can't let yourself be seduced by the false laurels of past accomplishment. Your last deal is done and behind you. A notch in your résumé: so what? Tomorrow is still tomorrow. You're only as good as you are right now, this moment, and moving forward.

Which is why SEALs also have this expression: "You have to earn your Trident every day."

The SEAL trident emblem, with its golden eagle clutching an anchor, trident, and flintlock pistol, is one of the most recognizable and most highly respected insignias in the military. I've seen commanding officers approaching in ship passageways step aside and let us through when they see that logo on our chests. It takes a lot to earn that Trident—but a big part of the SEAL ethos is that it isn't something you earn and then stick on your shelf, like an Oscar or an Emmy or an Olympic gold medal. A true SEAL knows he has to *keep* earning that distinction day in and day out. I've seen SEALs who forgot this golden rule and slacked off. They were removed from the community, along with their coveted Trident.

That's how I see being a CEO, which is why I've taken the old SEAL expression to heart in a new form in my new circumstance, a form that I think applies to any CEO, any director, any manager, any entrepreneur, any businessperson at any level of leadership: "You have to earn your title every day."

As I was about to learn once again.

At the start of 2015, looking at our totals from the year now behind us, I realized that I needed help. Professional help. No, not a therapist. A chief operations officer. There were too many things in the business that were getting out of control, that had already *gotten* out of control, including some I hadn't yet identified, let alone figured out how to fix. I knew enough to know that I didn't know what I didn't know. There was too much on my plate, and it was getting away from me. The Hurricane Group had grown to the point, in both size and complexity, where I couldn't keep managing it like a startup.

The problem was, I wasn't really being a CEO; I was being an *everything.* I had to focus. I had to earn my title back. And to do that, I was going to have to let go of managing everything—and start leading again.

It was time to delegate, big-time, and fast.

Recognize When It's Time to Delegate

When our first son was born, I was overseas; it was soon after 9/11, and my platoon was heading into Afghanistan, where I would stay until my deployment concluded in the spring of 2002 and I returned to the States. The first time I laid eyes on my son, he was already five months old. Seeing him for the first time was one of the most incredible experiences of my life.

But it was tough for my wife. She'd not only carried the little dude for the nine months before birth; she had also spent the past five months bonding with him. And now, letting this guy whom he'd never seen before pick him up? Hold him, walk around with him? Yes, I was his father, and yes, I was her husband. But she still had a hard time letting me take him. And you know, I understood that. This was *her* kid, and it was hard to hand him over to someone else.

Which perfectly describes how an entrepreneur feels handing over the reins to someone else for the first time.

In chapter 2, I talked about how crucial it is to stay on top of the details of your business—for example, doing the numbers yourself and not blithely handing them off to someone else. You can create big problems by rushing to delegate too soon. But you can also create problems by waiting too long to delegate. I've seen both situations, but in the balance I see far more problems come from people hanging on too long.

I've seen this happen up close, maybe fifteen times now: entrepreneurs who get to a certain level, typically just over a million in annual revenue, and run into a wall. They'll take their company to a certain level of success, where instead of being a struggling startup it's now something of a lifestyle business, but they just can't take it to the next level and turn the corner on scale. It isn't easy to relinquish control, to turn responsibilities over to others and let them run with it. But you have to do it.

That's what I had to do now.

This is going to be just like jumping out of an airplane, I told myself. *You're going to love it.* I can't say I was convinced I'd love it, but I knew it was time.

I jumped.

When I was in talks with the Scout Media people the previous spring, I had noticed that their chief revenue officer, Ben Madden, didn't seem that happy there. I knew Ben from *Maxim* magazine, which had printed a prepublication excerpt of my book *The Red Circle* when it came out in the spring of 2012. Ben was publisher at *Maxim,* and when it was sold in early 2014, Ben had gone over to Scout Media. In fact, Ben was how the people at Scout first learned about me and SOFREP.

Ben had a strong background in sales (in my business, *everyone* is a revenue generator) and I thought he would make a fantastic chief operations officer at Hurricane, so I got in touch. We started talking, and within days we had sketched out a deal that would bring him on board within the constraints of his current contract at Scout. Soon he was hired—and I was handing my baby over to someone else to hold.

Almost immediately, Ben started pointing out weaknesses in the operation, those blind spots I'd had an inkling were there but couldn't identify (because they were, well, blind spots). He also pointed out strengths I hadn't seen. He didn't just take a lot of the operational stuff off my plate; he took it off my plate and did it better than I could hope to.

He figured out that we had a technical problem with reporting that had resulted in more than two thousand subscribers who were active on the site but not paying. It took months to work out, but we finally tracked it down and fixed it. It was like finding tens of thousands of dollars in recurring monthly revenue hiding under the mattress, and we wouldn't have found it without Ben. In the final analysis, we collected almost $50,000.

He built up our three-person sales team to twelve, which had a huge impact almost immediately. He redid our whole marketing strategy. He had our home page redesigned. We locked in our company culture and created a vision of where we wanted to take the business, and we made sure everyone knew it inside and out.

It was as if I'd been running with ankle weights for months, and when I took them off, I couldn't believe how fast I could run. We started to grow again. I started thinking bigger and being more creative about the business's future. I took nearly a month off for that European trip, and Ben managed the whole team while I was gone. The house did not catch fire and burn to the ground. The business, if anything, thrived even more in my absence.

As an entrepreneur, you're going to wear twelve hats at first; that's just the way it is. You're going to learn a ton of different areas and tasks and skill sets, and that's essential. You *have* to know how all the pieces work. But once you're comfortable and have the knowledge, you need to start shedding responsibilities in order to increase your capacity to be more strategic and less tactical.

Bringing on a COO freed me up to *lead* again—to be charting the course for the future, and not just wrestling with the issues of the present.

Which led directly to an innovation that transformed our business model and added to our bottom line in a big way.

Embrace Disruption; Always Be Ready to Pivot

Leading from the front also means being out in front of the pack and staying out in front. Embrace innovation immediately, be an early adopter, have the courage to do things differently and take acceptable risks.

I was fortunate to learn this in the SEAL teams. One strong trait Navy SEALs have is that they're early adopters—both because of the nature of our work and because of the inherent personality types who wind up doing the work—and their quest for knowledge never ends. We're always looking out for the coolest new tools, the most advanced technologies, the latest developments in weapons and intelligence systems. Applying that same philosophy to business is crucial.

For example, in 2012 less than 20 percent of our traffic was on people's mobile devices. Today it's more than 90 percent. Which means we not only have to design all our Web sites to be mobile responsive but also that we needed to do that way back in our first year. (Which, fortunately, we did.) That's not the kind of change you can react to after the fact, because if you do, you've already lost a ton of your audience and you'll be playing a difficult—and possibly terminal—game of catch-up. (The first time I met with our editor for this book, Natalie, she said, "When we develop your title, we'll do a special thumbnail version of the front jacket, to make sure it's highly legible on mobile devices." I was impressed; that was the first time I'd heard an editor say that, and she was absolutely right.)

But adopting mobile responsiveness is a relatively minor technical issue compared with what happens when your entire business model is disrupted—which is what happened to us in 2015.

The online ad industry was changing. A lot of businesses were employing tactics that pumped up traffic with dummy pages that drove page views, but it wasn't real, and the moment they'd turn off the money pump, the traffic would die back down to an organic level. This drove ad rates down like crazy. Our CPM (cost per thousand clicks) rates started dropping like a rock, going from $30 or $40 down to a few dollars. Advertising agencies stopped caring about authentic traffic and audience engagement and started looking purely for scale. It created a race to the bottom; suddenly you had to have massive traffic to make any money in advertising. We were getting crushed.

Granted, we were not relying on advertising as much as we

had in the beginning, when advertising represented 100 percent of revenue; now it represented maybe 25 percent. But even that number was under attack now, and we couldn't build subscriptions fast enough to offset it.

When disruption happens, you can resist it, fight it, complain about it, even try to pretend it isn't happening . . . and doing any or all of the above will kill you as dead as Blockbuster, Polaroid, or Borders.

Or, you can embrace it—and pivot.

We pivoted.

We had already done this once, in the second half of 2013, when we changed our model and went to a paid subscription on SOFREP. It was a risky move, but it worked. Now we needed to pivot again.

The thing was, none of our traffic was artificially propped up by buying page views. All our traffic was organic; that is, it was *authentic*. Experts in the business looked at us and said, "Wow, your audience engagement is just off the charts." If we couldn't translate that into massive advertising revenue, maybe we could find some way to leverage it more authentically *and* more effectively.

It was actually our customers who gave us the idea. They were constantly asking us for recommendations and referrals on good equipment they could buy. Sometimes they would buy something from one of our advertisers and then feel as if they weren't well taken care of. The product would be inferior, or they'd gotten lousy customer service, and they'd come back to us and complain. This irritated me, both because I didn't like our customers not being treated well and because it reflected poorly on us. After being burned a few times, I became very cautious about which advertisers we were partnering with.

In late 2015, we held a major strategy meeting to talk about the future of the company, and during that meeting we started reviewing this whole advertising situation. We had pulled in a few of our advisory board members by conference call, and one of them spoke up and said, "Why don't you guys do a subscription box, like Birchbox, only with tactical gear?"

It was a brilliant idea. Rather than put advertisers in front of our audience and hope for the best, we could pick out the primo gear ourselves, so we could control the quality of the selection. Subscribers would pay monthly to become part of this community, where they could ask us questions and use us as a resource, as well as getting their monthly box; this would create a whole new level of audience engagement and satisfaction. We could deliver a quality consumer experience through great customer service and community building—and at the same time, we'd be creating a new revenue stream.

That conversation happened in November. By December, we were shipping our first batch of boxes. Within another two months, we took the Crate Club idea and used it to launch the SOFREP Book Club.

If we hadn't made those two pivots—the move to paid subscription in 2013 and the launch of our e-commerce box programs in 2015—I would be running a media company today worth tens of thousands instead of more than $100 million.

Which brings up an ancillary point: the only reason we were able to pivot so sharply and adopt totally new programs so smoothly and so rapidly was that we had extremely tight communication with the entire team.

Communicate with Your Team; Do It Well and Do It Often

During my four years in the navy before going into BUD/S, I did two separate six-month deployments to the Pacific, on two different aircraft carriers. These two deployments gave me one of the best lessons in leadership I've ever had.

The first deployment was on a modern, magnificent, nuclear-powered ship, the USS *Lincoln*. It was a nightmare—a six-month ordeal marked by petty politics, one-upmanship, and constant ob-structionism to my efforts at career advancement. The ship was un-kempt and dirty. Everyone was miserable. One helo exercise I participated in went haywire and came within inches of killing all four of the onboard crew (including me). By the time I reached the end of the six months, it felt like six years.

When the time came for my second deployment, I dreaded it. The ship I'd be on this time, the USS *Kitty Hawk*, was a convention-ally powered vessel that had been around since Vietnam. Oh, boy. If six months on the brand-new USS *Lincoln* was miserable, how much was this deployment going to suck?

Incredibly, it didn't suck at all. In fact, it was great. The place was clean and well organized, everything hummed along, and everyone was happy and productive. Morale was consistently high. The six months flew by. It blew my mind. And it wasn't hard to figure out what made the difference.

My first night aboard, I was surprised to hear the captain of the *Kitty Hawk* come over the PA loudspeaker, welcoming us and briefly outlining what would be happening the next day. I was amazed. Nothing like that had ever happened on the *Lincoln*. On that first deployment, the captain hardly ever talked to his crew. The captain on the *Kitty Hawk* not only talked to us that first night; he did so every single day for the full six-month stretch.

That was the difference. Not the vessel, not the equipment, not the staffing, but the fact that on one ship the captain never talked to us, and on the other he did.

It's such a simple thing: talk to your people, share the plan with them so they know where you're all heading and the purpose behind what you're doing. Engage your crew; have a dialogue; let them know that you know they exist and that they're part of what you're all doing together.

Don't leave your people in a vacuum.

I've often reflected on the lesson of the two captains, and there have been moments when I forgot it, too. There was a time at Hurricane when my philosophy was that I had all these talented writers and I should leave these guys alone and let them do their own thing. Respect their autonomy. Not get in their hair. I thought that was good leadership—but it backfired. After a while, I started getting feedback that the writers thought I was inaccessible and they didn't like it. When I asked them about this, they said, "No, man, we *want* to hear from you. We want to know what you're thinking."

Oops. Got it. Be the captain who communicates—not the one who doesn't.

Engage your people. Let them know what's going on. Talk to them. Keep them informed, and they'll stay involved. Treat them like the stakeholders they are.

Make Sure Everyone on the Team Knows Exactly What the Mission Is

The legendary management guru Peter Drucker based his consulting practice on five essential questions he said every business needed to ask and answer for itself. Of those five, the first was first for a reason: it was the most important. And it was just four words long: *What is your mission?*

What business are you in? What are you really doing, and why are you doing it? What is it you seek to achieve by doing it? What are your objectives? What kind of mark do you want to make on the world?

Drucker said an effective mission statement should be short and so clearly focused that it would fit easily on a T-shirt.

That sounds nice and neat in theory. The reality is often messier. As I mentioned in chapter 3, our mission at SOFREP changed during the course of our first few years. That happens. Ryan Zagata didn't get entirely clear on Brooklyn Bicycle Company's mission until a few years in.

So yes, it may take some time and effort, even struggle, to get clear on what the mission really is. Yet it's critically important that you strive to do so ASAP—because if you don't have a crystal clear and compelling mission, and communicate it clearly and effectively to everyone on your team, you're going to be like a batter at the plate swinging with his eyes closed. Sure, you *might* hit one of the balls pitched your way, but the odds aren't good.

Or to put it in sniper terms, hitting a target at a thousand yards, in the wind, is hard enough. How do you expect to do it when you can't even see the target? Doesn't matter how many times you pull the trigger or how good your weapon and ammo are. You're shooting blind.

Examine any great plan, and you'll find its genius lies in the simplicity of its stated objective. This ensures that everyone— *everyone*—understands the common goal.

This is our nation's biggest foreign-policy problem. For example, we've drifted in Afghanistan without a clear plan. Want proof? Just ask ten of your friends what our objective is in Afghanistan, and you're sure to draw ten different answers.

This is a serious problem. Anyone who has served in the military knows that having the entire team on the same page of music is critical for mission success. In this case, "the team" is the American public. If the public doesn't understand what we're doing abroad, then how can we make informed decisions and make sure our concerns are being represented by our elected officials?

You can't afford the luxury of such lack of focus in your business. Whatever your business's overall mission is, take the time and effort to put it into the clearest, most concise expression possible, and then make sure you communicate that clearly to everyone on the team. Ask yourself, "What are we doing? No, really: *What are we doing?* Why are we doing that? What's the point? What is it that we're trying to create through doing that?" Keep examining your purpose, peeling away the layers of the onion, until you get to the core of what you're up to. At SOFREP, our current mission statement is "Trusted news and intelligence from Spec Ops veterans."

Here is an e-mail I send out to every new team member when he or she first joins the team. It'll give you a sense of how we communicate our mission and culture at Hurricane:

MY HURRICANE GROUP ON-BOARDING LETTER

Congratulations and welcome to the Hurricane team! This letter lets you know three things about the company. Our history, our culture, and our vision.

One of my favorite books that showcases great leadership is called *Endurance,* the story of the famous explorer Ernest Shackleton and his incredible, fateful voyage to the Antarctic. By far one of the best books I've read on exemplary leadership under the harshest of conditions. How we recruit team members at Hurricane is very similar to the original advertisement Shackleton ran in a local London paper to recruit his team:

"Men wanted for hazardous journey. Low wages, bitter cold, long hours of complete darkness. Safe return doubtful. Honor and recognition in event of success."

Why is this relevant to you? Because working autonomously for our company is a challenging environment, one where you'll be expected to hold yourself accountable, both personally and to our entire team.

Please read this letter in full, and if you decide that this isn't the place for you, we'll give you $1,000 no questions asked and wish you the best.

Our History

In December 2011, I had a crazy idea for a new Web site called SOFREP—Special Operations Forces Situation Report—and pitched the idea to a few people I trusted, including Jack Murphy. At the time, Jack was finishing his degree at Columbia, having served time in the Army Rangers and Special Forces in Iraq, and I was working full-time as an executive at L3 Communications, having lost my first business and entire net worth a year earlier after transitioning out of the U.S. Navy SEAL teams. (Fun times.) We were both writing on the side and working part-time for a military content site, running a gear review blog.

Jack and I brought that blog from tens of thousands of page views to millions of page views in a very short time. Suddenly we were in a tie with the online property's largest blog, and it felt damn exciting—as if we were closing in on capturing bin Laden himself. I knew we were onto something big. At the time, there was a ton of interest out there in the world of Special Operations, but virtually nothing on the Internet. We had provided this window to many male fans through the blog, but I didn't own that site, and a lot of our ideas for growing and expanding content were shot down, which I attributed to a lack of solid culture and a massive bureaucracy—two things I can't stand.

Adversity often produces opportunity.

After I pitched Jack on the idea, and we spent a month of sleepless nights writing content and code for the site, we launched SOFREP on February 1, 2012. It took off right away, but I saw it as the start of something much bigger. We weren't going to just launch a single Web site. We were going to create a network of sites.

We grew, in more ways than one. SOFREP started as an information portal into the Special Ops community, but within a year it had grown organically into a serious foreign policy, military issues, and domestic security news site. This happened because the Special Ops veteran writers wanted to tackle big issues that the mainstream media were getting terribly wrong.

SOFREP also became a foundation for other sites and other content and then for our clubs. Since 2012, we have added a top-ranked podcast, SOFREP Radio; other content sites that cover guns, gear, reality TV, and military aviation; and our men's tactical gear club, the Crate Club. What Discovery Channel, Nat

Geo, and A&E's History channel do with their military content on cable TV, we do on the Internet. What Bass Pro Shop provides with its retail experience, we deliver with our e-commerce clubs.

Our Culture

My time in the SEAL teams taught me that most people are capable of ten times the output they accept as "normal." This doesn't mean I expect everyone to work like an ancient Egyptian pyramid slave worker! I say this only to provide a background for what you're getting into. In SOF, we look for intelligence, a can-do attitude, and people who are self-driven and who have several skill sets or just know how to get something done.

Because we are a media company, you will inevitably encounter gossip on the Internet about me and our business. Here is an important lesson I've learned: judge a person by his accomplishments and the company he keeps, not by rumors and the gossip mill. People who try to tear others down are often not in a very good place in their lives. We have been able to accomplish much in a short period of time, while others with greater resources and three-letter university degrees have not been able to execute successfully.

"Success requires no explanation; failure permits no alibis." —Napoleon Hill

Ben and I have an open-door policy. We ask only that you attempt to resolve a challenge within your team first, before reaching out to us.

Our core values outline the spine of our company culture at Hurricane. Company culture is extremely important to me; please read the list below and take it seriously. Consider it our

Constitution. Anytime you find yourself needing guidance in a difficult situation, you can reference our core values.

Hurricane Group Core Values

People First: We take care of our audience, sponsors, partners, friends, and family. This gives us a strong foundation in all we do.

Honesty and Integrity: Both are valued in everything we do, and we see doing the right thing and brutal honesty with each other and our customers as competitive advantages.

No Limits: We see endless possibilities to what we can create together. We are solution-based thinkers, welcoming new ideas and personal growth. Work smarter, not harder; we know the difference between "busy" and getting shit done.

We Give Back: We are committed to giving back to military and civic charitable causes that we care about. We want to leave the world a better place than we found it.

Our Vision

Not having a clear vision for your life or business is like taking a great voyage without knowing the destination. Sounds crazy, right? You'd be surprised at how many people and companies I've encountered who don't have a clear vision and just "go with the flow." If you don't define where you're going, you'll drift like a stick in a river and go wherever the current takes you.

Our vision as a company is simple: *We deliver amazing experiences with our content and products.*

Each year we create a vision theme for what we want to accomplish over that year, you'll be encouraged to share your ideas and contribute to this, because none of us is as smart as all of us, and to ensure a "safe return," we all need to work to-gether.

Remember, *the only easy day was yesterday.*—U.S. Navy SEALs

Welcome to the team.

Brandon Webb, Founder & CEO

And it's not just your overall mission that needs defining and communicating. In the course of business, you'll constantly be launching initiatives at the strategic or tactical level, and each of those initiatives has its own mission. For us, initiatives such as going to paid subscription, standing up a new Web site (or taking one down), and launching coverage of a particularly controversial story are all missions that I needed to make sure everyone on the team completely understood going in. For example, my specific vision statement for Hurricane for the coming year is this: "We are going to disrupt military news and television content with our online TV channel. We will become the best-in-class tactical gear club and No. 1 in category, while delivering incredible customer service across all channels—visitor, club member, vendor, and sponsor."

And by the way, that communication needs to go both ways, which brings us to the next critical point:

Don't Be Too Proud to Ask for Input

As important as it is to trust your own gut, it's just as important to remember that you are just one person with one opinion. Never confuse what *you* like, prefer, or want with what your market likes, prefers, or wants. What you think will sell or be attractive is not necessarily the best solution.

This is one reason you need to surround yourself with good people whose advice you can trust. Because you need more than just you. Look to your friends, colleagues, and associates for advice. Ask as many people as you can when surveying a new product, service, or idea. Get input from smart people you trust—and not necessarily people who think the same way you do or hold the same opinions you do. Invite challenge and diverse opinions. Take it all in. Then make your own informed decision.

As I said in chapter 6, we have a strong cultural bias in America toward the lone hero figure. From Horatio Alger to Steve Jobs, we love to tell the story of the lone guy battling the odds and carving success out of a wall of adversity. In the last few years, the American media have trained their hero-worship sights on the SEAL community in particular. Which, I grant you, is easy to understand. I've done it myself, putting out a book called *Among Heroes* that tells the story of eight SEALs I've known, all of whom I've learned from and after whom I model myself.

These men *are* heroes. But here's the critical point: that's not what they set out to do. Writers have a saying: "Only a fool sits down to write a masterpiece." (Elmore Leonard, one of the greatest crime writers of the twentieth century, said, "If I come across anything in my work that smacks of 'good writing,' I immediately strike it out.") When you sit down to write, you set out to do the best job you can. Period, full stop. That's what SEALs do. The moment you start *trying* to be a hero, you're not a warrior anymore. (I'm not sure what you are; maybe a politician.)

The truth is, SEALs prize teamwork. So do successful business leaders.

Every entrepreneur is a solo operator by nature, much like every Spec Ops warrior. Yet you cannot be a fully effective entrepreneur and hit over $2 million in revenue (that seems to be the magic differentiator) unless you know how to work as part of a team. This was something Steve Jobs taught himself, which is why his career wasn't over when he was canned from Apple in 1985. A good leader isn't one who always has (or thinks he has) the answers. A good leader is the one always asking the questions and being smart about *looking* for the answers.

As sniper instructors, my training partner Eric Davis and I learned that we were never finished learning and that our students could be a wealth of new information and insight for us. When graduates like Chris Kyle would come back from deployment in Iraq, we would invite them to come in, debrief, and make recommendations on how we could better train our students for the urban sniper environments they'd be facing. We actively sought out the same kind of knowledge from SEAL snipers returning from Afghanistan, Africa, and other not-so-friendly places and would then incorporate this information into our yearly curriculum review. If it seemed important enough, we'd make the change within weeks.

Being in the digital media arena, I see a lot of people who are in positions of importance, but who don't have a full grasp of all the technical issues involved, pull back from asking technical questions—for fear they'll betray their ignorance, I imagine. I have no problem betraying my ignorance. Some of this stuff is pretty arcane, and I'm not shy about asking for help understanding just what the hell it is we're doing. To me, saying "I don't understand, please explain" is not a sign of weakness; it's a demonstration of open-mindedness, intelligence, humility, and fearless leadership.

Listen to your customers, your team members, your employees, your financiers. Every one of them knows something you don't, and chances are it's something you need to know. And remember that the intern making the coffee may be in a position to see an answer to a question that the person sitting in the corner office hasn't thought about. Great leaders know this and are open to input from up and down the chain of command. Great leaders are secure in themselves. They know great ideas—winning ideas—can come from anyone and anywhere. They don't let rank or seniority dictate who has the best solution to a given problem. Leaders aren't afraid to surround themselves with people smarter than themselves.

Thanks to my friend (and excellent lawyer) John Tishler, I once had the honor of having lunch with Dr. J. Robert Beyster, the nuclear physicist who founded the billion-dollar company SAIC (Science Applications International Corporation). After lunch, we went back to his office, where I noticed a sign on his wall that spoke volumes about how he had achieved his level of success. It said, NONE OF US IS AS SMART AS ALL OF US.

Be Willing to Do the Grunt Work

I recently hired a guy, a former Army Ranger who'd gone back to school after leaving the service and had just graduated with his MBA. I brought him on as a consultant. "This is a trial period for you as well as for us," I explained. "You're trying us out, and we're trying you out."

He lasted three weeks.

He had applied for a position in operations, but it quickly became clear that he didn't really want to do the things involved in operations; he wanted to sit in an ivory tower and send out Power-Points with ideas and data analysis and not do the work itself. Ben told me that the guy actually said, "I have an MBA. I shouldn't be doing this petty stuff. I should be telling people what to do."

I told *him* what to do: hit the f'ing road, Jack. We quickly let him go, and I'm 100 percent positive we saved ourselves a whole lot of headache in doing so.

A great leader never asks his people to do anything he isn't willing to do himself. When we do a book event, we all pitch in afterward, emptying trash, breaking down the tables. I have no problem rolling up my sleeves and doing the grunt work; whatever needs doing. People see that and respect it. The only effective way to lead is by example. Be the one putting away chairs after the meeting.

That's the difference between a boss and a leader. A boss sits out back, whipping the troops on; a leader gets out in front of the line, urging troops to follow. The first barks orders and uses positional authority to intimidate; the latter sets the example and thus becomes the one whom others will willingly follow. I've seen many different leadership styles, but I've never seen anyone who leads from the rear gain the respect of the team. That's why this chapter, and the leadership style that inspired it, are both called "Lead from the Front."

When I was teaching at the SEAL sniper course, I worked for a terrible boss for a few sessions. Harvey treated his people very poorly, but in the military, chain of command is chain of command, and the boss is the boss. One Friday, at the conclusion of a three-month course, we all came back to our San Diego compound and put our gear away. I had the students do a quick cleanup, and then I sent both my staff and my students home shortly after noon so they could have a little more weekend to spend with their families. Most of these students would soon be rotating overseas to Iraq or Afghanistan, so I knew what even an extra half day off meant to them. And my instructors deserved the time off. I stayed behind to ready the office for Monday's graduation ceremony.

Early the next morning my phone rang. It was Harvey, steaming mad and screaming at me. The student lockers weren't up to his standards, and he wanted me to recall all my instructor staff to come back in and clean up. These were the same instructors, *his* instructors, who had just busted their asses for three months to put out some of the best snipers on the planet . . . and he was worried about a few messy lockers?

Yes, chain of command is chain of command—but I had a responsibility to my guys, and that came first.

I told Harvey there was no way I was doing that to my staff. I said I'd rather come back in and clean the entire cage area myself, if that's what he insisted on. I spent half my Saturday cleaning, missing out on time with my own family, so my staff wouldn't have to be away from *their* families. Word spread fast, and before I'd even finished the job, my instructors and students had all found out what happened. They knew I could have ordered them back on Saturday but instead chose to sacrifice my own weekend, and time catching up with my own family, for their benefit.

Which person do you think gained their respect: Harvey or me?

Never Lose Your Entrepreneurial Spirit

Unlike a lot of my Spec Ops friends, I don't come from a military family. There's no armed forces history in my bloodline, but there is a strong current of entrepreneurial blood on both sides of my family tree.

My grandmother Doris was forced into business when her husband, my mom's father, died early. He had supported the family as a milkman; now it was all on Doris. She started a collection agency, and when that went well, she bought a few more collection companies and ran the whole thing as a very successful business. I'd just been born, so she named her agency Brandon Tyler Associates (Tyler being my middle name).

If you're old enough to remember the 1980s television show *Remington Steele,* you'll get a kick out of this. In that show, a young woman (Stephanie Zimbalist) starts her own detective agency, but nobody wants to hire a female private eye, so she invents a fictitious male boss named Remington Steele. The plot heats up when Pierce Brosnan enters the scene, steps into Steele's shoes, and takes on his identity. That last part didn't happen to my grandmother, but she did choose a guy's name for her agency for the same reason as Stephanie Zimbalist. Now and then, someone would demand to speak with Mr. Tyler, and she'd just laugh and think, *If only you knew, buddy.*

My mom has always been entrepreneurial, too. She ran a restaurant with my father's sister and later started her own boat maintenance business, sanding and varnishing the boats and keeping the woodwork in good condition. She was the head cook on the dive boat I worked on in my teens and published her own cookbook for boaters, *The Galley Companion*. I remember how hard she worked on that thing and how much I enjoyed cooking with her as a kid in the tiny galley of our sailboat. She was and still is an inspiration to me.

As I said, my dad was my first model of the entrepreneurial life. When I was still young, I saw his business collapse around him and the toll that took on him, financially and emotionally. But here's the rest of the story: decades later he completely reinvented himself, hanging up his W2 job as a construction super and becoming a successful spec home builder and land developer. Last time I checked, he was a quarter of the way through a five-thousand-mile great-circle route on his boat via the Great Lakes and Caribbean, living life on his own terms.

Whether he knows it or not, my father taught me an important lesson: learn from your mistakes, and don't be afraid to chase your dreams no matter how old you are. I say this, because even with all the phenomenal learning that comes with the SEAL experience, and even with all the wisdom and savvy and excellent judgment I've been able to tap into through knowing the amazing businesspeople I've had the good fortune to meet in New York, through EO and our advisory board—even with all that, I think what has benefited me most in my own business life has been that model from my own family. I'm hoping I've been able to pass a bit of that on to you through these pages.

Being an entrepreneur, in my mind, isn't just about being the *literal definition* of entrepreneur, the person who creates his or her own startup company. Yes, that's an amazing journey. But that's the limited-definition version of entrepreneur.

Then there is the larger point: having an *entrepreneurial spirit*.

To me, it doesn't matter whether you have actually started your own business or are fulfilling a leadership role in a business you didn't start yourself: I believe there is an entrepreneurial spirit that anyone and everyone in any sort of leadership position needs to embody in order to do the job to its fullest.

By this wider definition, an entrepreneur is not a "business founder" but simply someone who *makes things happen*. Who doesn't wait to be told what to do, who doesn't sit around looking for someone else to take the initiative, who doesn't simply fulfill the task he's handed and then stop. Having entrepreneurial spirit means that you are always looking for ways to fulfill the Olympic motto, *Citius, Altius, Fortius*—"Faster, Higher, Stronger!"—always looking for ways to do something better, serve more people and serve your existing customers better, take a new and more profitable or more productive path, provide a kind of value no one has ever provided before.

A director, manager, customer service agent, restaurant waitstaff— hell, *anyone* engaged in any place of business can play an entrepreneurial role in building and growing and perfecting that business. You don't have to literally own a business to *own* it. What's more, all successful business owners I know started out, at some point in their past, as employees in someone else's business, exceptional cogs in someone else's wheel, who took pride and pleasure in carving excellence out of the place they were positioned. George Washington started out as a land surveyor, Sam Walton as a waiter. Whatever role you happen to occupy, either you are leading by example—or you're not.

Having an entrepreneurial spirit means you don't just do a job; you take pride in it, pour yourself into it, give it your heart and soul and, yes, your total focus, and in so doing, you find ways to elevate the enterprise. It means you invest the business with excellence; you invest it with *yourself.*

I've shared our vision as a company; I thought I'd include my own personal vision statement here, too. As a leader, I think it's important to know who you are—and who you aspire to be.

I live an adventurous and meaningful life. I value time as my most precious asset and use it wisely. I plan my life and live my plan.

I speak candidly and respect people's views and choices. I don't fall prey to certainty. I lead by example.

I stay physically fit and eat healthy. I set challenging goals and achieve them. I never give up, and I know the difference between failing and quitting.

I see fear and adversity as necessary opportunities to grow and learn. I am always striving to learn and improve myself as a father, friend, son, companion, and business leader to my team.

I am leaving the world a better place.

PROFILE: MATT MEEKER
(BARKBOX)

I met Matt through my good friend Nick Ganju, cofounder of Zocdoc. In early 2016, when we were starting the subscription part of the business and trying to work through some logistic challenges, Nick said, "You should talk to Matt. He's been through this." We met and became quick friends. His input has been invaluable to our development of the Crate Club and Book Club programs.

A Minnesota boy, Matt looks every bit the part: mild mannered, soft spoken, typically dressed in plain jeans and plaid shirt. But don't let that genial nature fool you: Matt is an animal (and, yes, pun intended) who has spent his whole career at the forefront of disruption and innovation.

Emerging from college in 1997, he was uninspired by the Fortune 500 companies showing up at the job fairs—but he was intrigued with the Internet. None of these companies were talking about that back then (or even thinking about it), so he went looking for an opening at a smaller company, as he says, "something where I could learn faster and get my hands a little dirtier."

He found a digital ad agency in New York that was hiring young people who were hungry to learn. In 1997, the very concept of a digital ad agency was radical, and when Matt packed his bags and moved to New York, it was like crossing the continent in a covered wagon and stumbling upon giant redwoods and the Pacific Ocean. The company, i-traffic, played with all sorts of unlikely concepts like pay-per-click that today are taken for granted. Matt and his colleagues created the first banner ad. ("So, yeah," he says. "We're the ones to blame for that.") They also helped introduce clients like Disney, Staples, Capital One, and Discover card to the untapped horizons of the Internet, helping them get online and learn how to navigate their presence on this unknown space called the World Wide Web.

After two years, the company was sold to a large, traditional agency, and Matt decided to hit the bricks. For the next few years, he worked on an idea for a handheld communication device built into a credit card—prescient stuff back in those pre-smart-phone days when texting wasn't yet a thing. He and his business partner burned through $15 million without releasing a single product. Matt says he learned some critical lessons in that failed venture that would serve him well later. (More on that shortly.)

His next business idea was triggered, in a way, by the events of 9/11. He and a friend, Scott Heiferman, were struck by the feeling of community in New York City in the days after the attacks. People were talking to each other, meeting up in coffee shops, showing genuine concern for one another. Inspired by what they saw, Matt and Scott started asking themselves, "How could we create that more permanently, and all around the world?"

That question led them to start Meetup.com, an online portal dedicated to helping people find and meet other people who share common interests. They formed the company in January 2002 and launched the site that June.

Meetup was a phenomenal success, in terms of its growth and popularity, but it also offered a years-long laboratory in the challenge of how to monetize a digital business (a challenge we would grapple with a decade later at Hurricane Group). For the first few years, they tried various business models, but nothing stuck.

In April 2005, after three years in the business, Matt was touring the country to meet members and organizers and listen to their product requests. At a meeting in Atlanta, a woman stood up and said, "I'm so glad you're here. I joined the Atlanta Breast Cancer Survivors Meetup four months ago. I've been struggling to recover and was really looking forward to this group meeting—but it's been four months, and so far there hasn't been a single event. I'm starting to lose hope."

Her story hit Matt hard. This was a problem they'd been wrestling with for a while now. Because anyone could start a Meetup group for free, they had tons of people starting groups and then doing nothing with them. All these groups lying dormant with members piled into them and nothing happening was creating bad experiences for people.

EBay founder Pierre Omidyar, who was on their board of advisers, had told them they needed to start charging their organizers a fee. "Most people who get to start a group for free won't take it seriously," he said. "This is a privilege you're offering them. You've invested a lot in this platform. You're providing value here. You need to charge."

For months, they had resisted his advice, but the woman in Atlanta added a whole new dimension to the issue. "This wasn't about Pokémon cards or knitting," says Matt. "This woman had her life hanging here by a thread, she was counting on this group—and someone had just started it and walked away."

That's when they decided Omidyar was right: they needed their people to have some skin in the game. They announced that they were going to start charging a monthly fee to host a Meetup group.

All hell broke loose. People screamed at them, flamed them, said they'd been betrayed, kicked and yelled, told them they were going to be out of business in no time. "They said just about every awful thing someone could say to you," says Matt.

Pierre had predicted that they would lose 85 percent of their user base, and he was close: they lost about 80 percent. "It was terrifying," says Matt.

It took about a month to go through the storm and emerge out the other side, but emerge they did. Not only did the new fee structure stabilize things and greatly increase user satisfaction, it also turned out to be a revenue model that made sense, and it's worked for them ever since. By 2008, the company was showing a profit, and it's still growing today.

After leaving Meetup in 2008 ("I felt like I'd done what I set out to do there"), Matt created a few more startups and had more or less settled down into an advisory role when he quite unexpectedly got bitten once more by the entrepreneurial bug.

He never planned to start Bark & Co. In fact, he resisted the idea. But he couldn't help it: he had a great idea. Or really, it was more like the idea had him. "I had no choice," he says. "It just dragged me in." (Think Al Pacino in *The Godfather: Part III*, only in corduroys.)

Matt had a dog he loved to spoil, a 130-pound Great Dane named Hugo. He was having a hard time finding new products for Hugo, so one day in the fall of 2011 he came up with this idea: a monthly box filled with treats and cool toys for dogs.

"It wasn't meant to be a big idea," he says. "It was just a side project, a little experiment to set up and watch, and make my dog happy along the way."

He told a friend, Henrik Werdelin, about the idea and Henrik sketched up a mock home page, which Matt set as his cell phone home screen. He started showing it to friends to see what they thought. People said, "Hey, that's great—I have a dog, so let me know when it's live, and I'll sign up!" After a few weeks of this, Matt attached a Square credit card reader to his phone and started taking orders—for a product that didn't exist, for a company that didn't yet exist either. By December, he had forty-nine paying customers eager to start their subscriptions.

The holidays were just around the corner. Matt and Henrik figured they better come up with something soon to satisfy those people who'd voiced their interest and put up their credit cards, so they hastily assembled some items into some boxes and shipped off forty-nine packages.

They've shipped every month since.

By the end of the first year, they'd gone from those first 49 to about 10,000 customers. By the end of year two, it was 60,000, and it kept growing. By the end of 2015, they were at about 225,000 monthly shipments, and in 2016 they doubled that to about 450,000. By the time this book is in the stores, they'll be at well over half a million BarkBox customers.

In March 2014, *Forbes* named BarkBox No. 4 on its list of "20 Companies You Should Be Following on Social Media"—a list that included TED Talks, SpaceX, Starbucks, and Zappos. Not too shabby.

Even as their core concept, the BarkBox, has continued to grow like crazy, Matt and his partners have continued spinning off new idea after new idea. Just as I've found with our Web sites, some of those ideas stick and some don't. The BarkPost, a blog about dogs (sort of a dog-themed BuzzFeed), and BarkShop, a retail portal for pet-related products, are both alive and thriving as I write this. Bark-

Care, a virtual veterinary referral service complete with twenty-four-hour hotline for dog questions and emergencies (and even house calls), didn't make the cut, and they had to shutter it after a year.

All grist for the entrepreneurial mill.

Right now they're working on BarkAir, an ambitious plan to provide a door-to-door travel experience, partnering with ride-sharing companies, hotels, and airlines. The week we held our interview, they were doing a trial flight from New York to Boston with a complement of dogs.

Which brings me to the point of Mr. Meeker's Wild Ride and the critical lessons Matt says he's learned along the way. The success of Bark, especially as placed side by side with the colossal failure of that early tech company that never shipped a product, has shown Matt three keys to staying out ahead of the curve and doing so successfully:

1. *Don't overfund, overthink, or overplan.* "We had too much money," says Matt of his doomed 2000 company, which had a $15 million budget and no product. At Bark, they had a product shipping before they had anything else. The lesson: Build the idea first. Ship a product. If the idea is solid, the money will follow, and so will the planning. The key is to plant your flag and make something real happen.

2. *Get your idea out in front of people.* Real, live customers are the most important source of business intelligence you have. Get your idea out in front of them right away. Never allow yourself to become isolated from the voices of end users. Listen to your customers, and let them guide you.

Matt had access to the wisdom of Pierre Omidyar, one of the most successful digital entrepreneurs of his generation—but it was contact with that woman in Atlanta who drove the wisdom home. And it was customer response, even before they'd shipped a product, that told Matt and Henrik they had a viable business.

3. *Keep it fresh.* Don't let your company get stale and "established." Give your people the freedom to create, to innovate, to come up with new ideas and new products. At Bark, some of the new ideas have come from the business owners, some from employees, and some from customers. They keep passing the baton of leadership back and forth.

"Which is difficult," says Matt. "As a perfectionist, it's tough to let go, to let other people take your thing and run with it. But there's tremendous power in that, too."

I thought I should close this chapter by telling you how we did in getting out of that 2014 slump.

I brought Ben on at the beginning of 2015, and we immediately did some housecleaning and restructuring. I also decided it was time to stop this commuting silliness and put myself in the belly of the beast, so I secured a small rental in the heart of Manhattan and relocated from California and Nevada to New York City and San Juan, Puerto Rico (for the tax advantages and fantastic climate). During 2015, Ben and I put together an advisory board of outstanding businesspeople from a wide range of fields whom we could tap to help us with our thinking: people like Betsy Morgan, Kamal Ravikant, and Matt Meeker. In November, we held that strategy meeting where we decided to create our own box-subscription program.

We launched the Crate Club in January 2016 and the SOFREP Book Club a few months later. In January 2016, we also made a huge jump in the volume of our content on SOFREP, increasing from three or four posts a day to twenty or more as a tactic to increase traffic to the site. This also had the effect of cementing us as a solid source for news and current events.

We finished 2015 at about $1.5 million in top-line revenue. In 2016, we had already sailed past the million mark by April; we closed out the year at $4.5 million and will grow to almost ten times that in 2017—with fewer than sixteen people on the team.

Here's what happened, in a nutshell: I stopped being simply busy and started being effective again. I got back to leading with a clear vision—and leading from the front.

CONCLUSION

✧ ● ✧

One spring day in early 2000, my best friend, Glen, and I got a call that we were wanted in our officer in command's office. Now. We hoofed it up there and found not only Jim McNary, our OIC, but also Tom, our platoon LPO (leading petty officer), and Dan, our chief petty officer, standing by Lieutenant McNary's desk. It was obvious that something major was up. Were we in some trouble? If so, we figured, it must be the big kind.

"Listen, guys," said Lieutenant McNary. "We're short on snipers. We want you two to go to sniper school."

Sniper school?! The idea of becoming a sniper had never occurred to me. Furthest thing from my mind, actually. I'd been a rescue swimmer and loved the water. I loved flying and had always wanted to be a pilot. But . . . a sniper? Hell, I'd never even handled a gun until I'd enlisted in the navy, and the navy (unlike the army and the marines) was not noted for its firearms training. As far as shooting weapons went, I was practically a virgin.

Plus, Glen and I were new guys. There were seasoned SEALs

who had waited years to get one of those coveted Naval Special Warfare sniper school slots and sure weren't going to be too happy about two snot-nosed young 'uns getting those billets ahead of anyone else. When those same seasoned SEALs heard that these two dipshit new guys were attending the course, they would no doubt be expecting us to fail and wash out, and they would probably be right.

Four years later, I was running the course.

This is what happens when you're an entrepreneur. One day you're wiping down the counters at the diner, and the next you're opening a chain of restaurants up and down the coast. It's a natural progression: total focus → excellence → leadership.

I served in the U.S. Navy for thirteen years, six months, and six days, most of that time in the SEAL teams but also for a few years before that as a helicopter aircrew search-and-rescue swimmer and airborne sensor operator (active and passive sonar, mostly). During that time, I experienced leaders from great to mediocre to terrible, some who nearly got me killed and some who almost certainly saved me from being killed. I served under leaders who inspired courage, loyalty, and outstanding performance from those they led, and others who inspired little but scorn. I'm happy to say the good far outnumbered the bad, but they all taught me valuable lessons.

I have been out of the service and on the battlefield of business now for close to the same length of time: eleven years, one month, and nine days as this book hits the bookstore shelves. During these years, I've built a multimillion-dollar startup that blew up in my face and brought me to my knees, and another multimillion-dollar startup that survived its early struggles and now stands tall as, if not a fully grown adult, at least a strong and healthy adolescent charging toward adulthood. During these years, I have leaned heavily on the experience and wisdom of business leaders whose savvy, good judgment, and sterling character remind me of the finest officers I've known.

Now that I've transitioned from SEAL to CEO, I often look back at my time in the military and my time in the business world and consider carefully what both have taught me about what it means to be a better leader.

When you're in a leadership position, you are the one who has to make the impossible decisions—and yes, typically under insane pressure. A smart leader does so only after listening to the people he or she trusts without question, that loyal inner circle of proven teammates, taking in all the feedback possible from as many different trusted perspectives as possible—but still the decision itself rests on one person's shoulders.

Being in a leadership position is not easy. You'll take plenty of shots from the cheap seats, and some of those shots may be loaded for bear. When that happens, it may help to know that it happens to the best among us. It simply comes with the territory—which is to say, with the responsibility. And like a blade on a good whetstone, it makes you sharper.

You'll fail, probably more than once. That, too, is not only inevitable but a positive force, guiding and propelling you forward. Failure seems to be a necessary ingredient in the humility and wisdom it takes to succeed greatly. No successful person I know has not failed, often greatly, along his or her way to great success. Don't let those failures dim your light or keep you down—and sure as hell don't listen to the critics, especially the ones who've never dared, who've never put their own skin in the game and name on the line.

Theodore Roosevelt, no stranger to slings and arrows from smaller men, said something about critics that has become one of my guiding quotations:

> *It is not the critic who counts; not the man who points out how the strong man stumbles, or where the doer of deeds could have done them better. The credit belongs to the man who is actually in the arena, whose face is marred by dust and sweat and blood; who strives valiantly; who errs, who comes short again and again, because there is no effort without error and shortcoming; but who does actually strive to do the deeds; who knows great enthusiasms, the great devotions; who spends himself in a worthy cause; who at the best knows in the end the triumph of high achievement, and who at the worst, if he fails, at least fails while daring greatly, so that his place shall never be with those cold and timid souls who neither know victory nor defeat.*

In those thirteen years plus in the military and eleven years plus in business, maybe the most important thing I've learned about leadership is this: It is not some special talent or skill, some inborn ability or exceptional capacity that makes you a leader. It certainly isn't an expensive education, high station, or family name that makes you a leader. It isn't even necessarily past accomplishments. What makes you a leader, more than anything else, is that you dare to plant your flag in the ground and do something nobody has done or is willing to do. A leader goes first. A leader charts the uncharted.

Leaders *lead*. It's that simple.

I started this book by telling you about the $15 million acquisition offer we got for Hurricane in 2014. We've had a few more offers since then, including interest from both A&E and IAC, the company that owns the *Daily Beast,* Tinder, and Match.com (among others). In the spring of 2016, we had four serious inquiries within 120 days. I haven't bit down on anything yet . . . but that doesn't mean it couldn't happen.

My perfect offer would look like this: A strategic (to us) company invests in us for a large stake and a fair valuation (we are well over the $100 million mark by now), and then leaves the team and me to keep running and building the business to a valuation of over a billion, as long as we keep hitting our metrics, for as long as I want to. Which I do until I get bored and decide it's time to put my focus on something else. Probably something that benefits humanity and stokes my passion for adventure.

And you? What does your vision or ideal scenario look like? If there's one thing I've learned about targets, it's that you're never going to hit yours if you don't know what—or where—it is.

I have no doubt that there is a great deal more I don't know, a vast amount still to learn, than what I have learned so far. But I do know this: Time is too precious to waste it in playing small. *Life* is too precious to waste it in playing small. Whatever excites you, intrigues you, stirs your passion, I urge you to go chase it *now*.

Here is what I've learned on the field of battle, both as a SEAL and as a CEO:

Stay focused—
Keep keenly attuned to everything going on around you—
Practice violence of action—
Hold fast to a standard of absolute excellence—
Embrace the suck—
Honor and value your team—
Lead from the front—

. . . and you'll do great things. *Spend yourself in a worthy cause.* I'll be here, cheering you on.

ACKNOWLEDGMENTS

※ ❀ ※

Building a book is like building a business: the idea may start with you, but its real-world success rests on the shoulders of the team you put together. My appreciation, gratitude, and respect go:

To my awesome co-author, John David Mann. John and I started working together on our first collaboration, *The Red Circle*, way back in 2009, when I was still in the midst of the Wind Zero effort, and right from the word "go" we talked about writing a book together on Spec Ops principles as applied to the world of business. John is not only a hell of a writer, he's also a hell of an entrepreneur himself.

To our fiercely talented literary agent, Alyssa Reuben, and her ace assistant at the Paradigm Talent Agency, Katelyn Dougherty, who helped this project find the most excellent home imaginable.

To our phenomenal publishing team at Portfolio: Natalie Horbachevsky, Bria Sandford, Leah Trouwborst, Kaushik Viswanath, Will Weisser, and Adrian Zackheim; you guys are the best there is at what you do, and I'm proud to join your catalog of business authors.

To Joe Apfelbaum, Solomon Choi, Matt Meeker, Betsy Morgan,

Kamal Ravikant, Amit Verma, and Ryan Zagata, for your generosity, your friendship, and your awesome stories.

To Randy Kelley, for forcing me to do my own numbers.

To the All-Star Brent Burns, No. 88 of the San Jose Sharks, for your friendship and the Stanley Cup memories; my dad and I will never forget the experience.

To my mom, Lynn; my dad, Jack; my grandmother Doris; and Grandma Barbara and Grandpa Jack for the entrepreneurial environment you all created for me, whether or not you knew you were doing so at the time!

To my amazing children, who continue to inspire me every day by pursuing your own paths.

To my incredible executive team at the Hurricane Group: Drew Dwyer, Adam Haddad, Anna Hughes, Desiree Huitt, Jason Kenitzer, Ben Madden, Angie Mobarak, Jack Murphy, Ian Scotto, Cris Tagupa, and Drew Wallace—and I'm sure there will be more of you by the time this book hits the bookstore shelves!

To our advisory board at Hurricane: Frank Farrell, George Kollitides, Sean Lake, Bill Ludwig, Sally Lyndley, Matt Meeker, Betsy Morgan, Kamal Ravikant, and Will De Rose, for your wisdom and guidance.

To the members of Entrepreneurs' Organization, New York City chapter, for being there for me when I needed it most.

And finally, to you, the one reading these words, for having the courage and dedication to walk the path. I hope you'll share this book with those people in your sphere of influence who will get the message and do something with it!

Spread the word: *Excellence matters.*

APPENDIX:
THE SEVEN PRINCIPLES

✦ ✦ ✦

1. Front Sight Focus

If I had to pick a single core principle for success in business, it would be this: choose one thing, focus on that one thing, and execute it to the absolute limit of your abilities. Focus on your business, invest in yourself, and learn how to say no to everything else.

- Stay on target; stay focused.
- Live every day with a single bullet.
- Embrace a state of healthy obsession.
- Win first in your mind.
- Pay attention to your self-talk.
- Master distractions.
- Communicate effectively and efficiently.
- Know your number.
- Get clear about money.
- Keep your balance.

2. Total Situational Awareness

The SEAL's obsession with training has its counterpart in business: the constant and relentless quest for knowledge. Become a ravenous observer of everything in your field. Nothing ever goes according to plan—first rule of battle, first rule of business—so be prepared for *anything*.

- Plan, look, listen.
- Pay attention.
- Practice using your peripheral vision.
- Stay thirsty.
- Know more than you think you need to know.
- Learn from the best.
- Don't trust conventional wisdom.
- Know your business's numbers.
- Stay flexible.
- Make sure you're in love with what you do.

3. Violence of Action

Do your homework, take every possible factor into account, focus unwaveringly on your target—and once the instant for action appears, act boldly and without hesitation. Operate with a bias for action. A good plan violently executed *now* is better than a perfect plan executed next week.

- Get off the *X*.
- Take the shot.
- Make action your default mode.
- Create action-focused work habits.
- Never use money (or lack of money) as an excuse.
- Be confident—not arrogant.
- Plan for disaster so it won't be a disaster when it happens (because it *will* happen).
- Don't be afraid to pull the plug.

4. Excellence Matters

Your commitment to excellence, or lack thereof, defines who you are as an individual. It dictates how you perform when everyone is watching, but it is also the standard you set for yourself when no one is looking. Excellence isn't simply a means to an end. It's a way of life—and business.

- Ask yourself, why are you in business?
- Have a thirst for excellence.
- Excellence is a state of mind.
- Hire the best.
- Improve constantly.
- Never settle.
- Put yourself in an environment of excellence.
- Upgrade your sphere of friends.
- Embody excellence.
- Strive for excellence in every aspect of your life.
- Know that excellence comes at a cost.

5. Embrace the Suck

A genuine commitment to excellence is impossible without a deep appreciation of pain and failure. Most outrageously successful business ideas are born out of the experience of failure, sometimes even bitter failure. The pain is temporary; the learning is priceless.

- There's gold within the muck.
- Make adversity your friend.
- Don't react—adapt and thrive.
- Take it one piece at a time.
- Look for clarity from the crisis.

6. One Team, One Fight

No matter what your business model or your industry, people are key to your success. Having the right people is far more important than having the right tools, technology, or financing. A team with average ability but great chemistry will win out over a team with extreme talent but lousy chemistry. Character counts more than talent, and attitude counts more than skill.

- Treat your people like family.
- Take hiring seriously.
- Hire people who fit your culture.
- Don't wait long to fire someone who isn't working out.
- Become an excellent judge of character.
- Reward people the way *they* want, not the way *you* want.
- Choose business partners as carefully as a marriage partner.
- Treat your customers like family, too.
- Put trust and loyalty in front of everything else.

7. Lead from the Front

Don't be seduced by the false laurels of past accomplishment. Your last deal is done and behind you, a notch in your résumé. Tomorrow is still tomorrow. You're only as good as you are right now, this moment, and moving forward. Remember the difference between a boss and a leader: A boss sits out back, whipping the troops on. A leader stays out in front, urging the troops to follow.

- You have to earn your title every day.
- Recognize when it's time to delegate.
- Embrace disruption; always be ready to pivot.
- Communicate with your team; do it well and do it often.
- Make sure everyone on the team knows exactly what the mission is.
- Don't be too proud to ask for input.
- Be willing to do the grunt work.
- Never lose your entrepreneurial spirit.

INDEX